DAILY DOUBLES 2

Celebrity Impersonators

C.J. MORGAN

AND

JACK BULLARD

Daily Doubles 2: Celebrity Impersonators
By C.J. Morgan and Jack Bullard

Published by:

Top Ten Productions
Nashville, Tennessee

Cover & Interior Book Design by Daniel Middleton and Naomi Middleton
Scribe Freelance | www.scribefreelance.com

Clarissa McNair as Editorial consultant

Second Edition

ISBN: 979-8-218-03058-2

Published in the United States

This book is dedicated to the memory of Bea Fogelman who promoted, supported and inspired us all.

Table of Contents

Foreword

MAGINE IF YOU WILL, going through your daily life having perfect strangers giving you *that look*, and every place you go, you look up to see people whispering under their breath, their faces filled with bewilderment and wonder . . . *"is that her?"*

It seems like a harmless kind of life moment, that is, until you find yourself bombarded with strangers snapping photos, and selfies, or requests for an autograph on a daily basis.

This experience can turn into hearing stories of how *you are their favorite actor*, and they have seen all your movies. This *looking like someone famous* can become a blessing in disguise, getting front row tickets to a season basketball game or the nicest seat in the house of an upscale restaurant.

This magical, mystery ride of working as a professional Celebrity Impersonator, Tribute Artist and Celebrity Lookalike has been a unique and un-tapped art form that has continued to unfold and establish itself as legitimate entertainment in the eyes of Hollywood since the early 1980's.

Casting directors, show producers, special event companies, and even celebrities themselves have come to rely on these *doppelgangers* to perform and even replace celebrities for all kinds of performances such as body doubles, voice over work, stand-in's, for film & TV, stage shows and even your everyday birthday party.

The unique, brave and talented artists you are about to meet in this book, will allow you a glimpse of what it is like to go through life with an iconic look, a well-known and recognized style or uncanny voice with a catch phrase that instantly provokes a smile everywhere you go.

Step into their shoes for a moment, and see what life is really like under the spotlight and through the lenses of *The Lookalike*. You will see not only the dedication, commitment, strength and determination it takes to succeed in this ever-changing industry, but you will also see the heart, comradery, and community it offers.

Working in this industry can offer experiences one can only dream about, allowing, offering and sometimes requiring travel to far off destinations or meeting people one may never get an opportunity to meet otherwise.

I am honored and blessed to have experienced and been a part of this incredible community for the past 28 years. Because of my work as both an impersonator and agent, I have been able to connect and share my experiences and continue my journey as a lookalike expert and coach. It has changed not only my life, but my destination, and all the lives I have encountered along the way.

I am grateful to be a part of this wonderful collection of Lookalike books by *C.J. and Jack* and more so, to call them friends, all thanks to the world of Lookalikes.

I hope you enjoy this book and each of the incredible stories of talented artists, as many have spent years working tirelessly to perfect their act and have now paved the way for future generations of talented performers—Each of them—a legacy of their own!

—DENISE BELLA VLASIS
Agent and author of *Made You Look: Who Do You Look Like?* Thrillennium Books, 2000
and *You've Got The Look: The Complete How to Celebrity Look-Alike Guide,* Trafford Publishing 2003

SECTION 1
The Art Form

O NE OF THE DICTIONARY definitions of the word impersonate is: To imitate the appearance, voice or manner of, to mimic. Another definition is: To embody, personify.

Some entertainers have developed this into artistry, blending our culture's fascination with celebrity into a highly specialized niche of show business.

Celebrity impersonators, including tribute artists and lookalikes, have become a very popular and viable part of the entertainment landscape. They have always been around, of course, but as the top tier of bona fide stars becomes more and more exclusive, elusive and expensive, the public is eager to see a reasonable facsimile.

Doubles have been standing in for stars since the golden age of movies, doing stunts and taking risks the stars would never take. They may play concerts, venues and clubs the celebrities would never play, always playing second fiddle, as it were, to the original. How does this affect the performer? How does one prepare for this rather unusual career choice? What does it take to be successful at this line of work?

Whether a tribute band or a dead-ringer for a living or a dearly departed actor or actress, politician or sports figure, the world of professional celebrity impersonators is at once strange, fun and fascinating. Some performers are the natural doppelgangers of the rich and famous. Others have mastered the art of disguise, including hair, make-up and wardrobe down to the last detail. They can project the image of sometimes not just one, but a number of different characters. Some have perfected not just the look but the sound and/or voice of legendary superstars, past and present.

An issue of *Playbill Magazine* once featured an interview with British actor Michael Sheen.

He portrayed the late talk show host David Frost in the Broadway play "Frost/Nixon," and also portrayed Tony Blair in the movie "The Queen."

"I think playing a real life person brings challenge over and above what you have to do with a fictional character—the extra work you have to do and how specific you have to be about the research. You have all the normal things you have to deal with when you play a character, where you have to tell the story and try to work out what the writer is intending. But you also have a responsibility to this actual person, in terms of trying to find out what they're all about."

"I read reviews where critics write, 'So-and-so plays this character without resorting to impersonation, as if impersonation is a really bad thing or it's cheating somehow. If you're playing a real person, you've got to be like him. That's the whole point. You don't have free reign to do whatever you want. I suppose impersonation means just doing the stuff on the exterior. But what's happening on the surface is often an expression of what's going on underneath. So, in some ways, the closer you get on the outside, the more that can help bring out what's going on under the surface. The two should be connected, really."

A professional, high-quality celebrity impersonator or tribute artist can create excitement and interest, generate publicity and attendance, help to establish a theme, create special moments and generally add fun to any event. For instance, Martha Stewart, a television personality who has created an empire based on home and garden, often features roses on her show. She has proudly displayed her rose garden, demonstrated pruning techniques and even made paper roses. Sharon Holmes, a Martha Stewart lookalike, offers a Martha-style rose ceremony for corporate award and recognition events and even birthdays. She honors individuals by handing out delicately decorated roses. A Dolly Parton tribute artist teaches audience participants how to play the 'spoons.' A presidential George Bush plays the guitar.

They take photos with guests, mingle with the crowd, act as emcees, hosts or hostesses. They film commercials, perform shows and mini-shows with bands or with tracks. Often they're asked for autographs (signing their own names, nicknames or sometimes just the first name of the celebrity they portray). They can do anything from serving as a photo double on a movie set to offering singing telegrams. Sometimes lookalikes will be hired for photo shoots, which some equate to modeling. However, even then, as Michael Cairns, a portrait photographer in Orlando, Florida points out, "Anyone who hopes to work as a lookalike must use the correct facial expressions, move your body the way they do, display mannerisms and certain trademark characteristics, such as a pout or a specific pose, even for still photos."

Some tribute artists offer shows with production values that rival the original artists, complete with dancers, props, sets and full bands. Often a show is built around a variety of celebrity impersonators such as the infamous *Legends in Concert* shows produced by John Stewart. Others headline an act that pays tribute to a single celebrity such as Neil Diamond, Frank Sinatra or Marilyn Monroe.

Some portray their character from a distinct time period; for instance, young Elvis from the late '50s or Barbra Streisand from the *Funny Girl* era. Others present a caricature of many different celebrities and play it for laughs. Canadian Bonnie Kilroe lampoons at least 20 different stars in her one-woman show, from Julie Andrews to Sharon Osbourne.

"As an actor, you're used to putting on characters, taking them off, becoming someone else, doing your research, and working on that." —Angela Bassett

---

These entertainers often put in long hours out on the road, paying homage to the likes of Johnny Cash, Cher and, of course, Elvis, in nightly shows. Some sing. Some don't. Sometimes it depends on the job itself. It is not unusual for any of them to spend thousands of dollars on authentically detailed costumes, wigs, props and instruments in order to accurately portray their superstar counterparts. The true professional does not simply don a cheap wig or a Halloween costume and pronounce him or herself a tribute artist or impersonator.

In many ways, being a tribute artist, impersonator or lookalike can be far more challenging than a scripted performance with a director at the helm. In this line of work, improvisational skills are a necessity and not everyone has them. You must be "in character,' sometimes for hours, depending on the situation. You must think and react the way the character would react, on the spot.

Who are these people who seem to be leading a double life? Are they entertainers in their own right? Are they fans? Have they met their celebrity counterparts? They are certainly often the recipient of scrutiny and many curious stares from a public who constantly compares them to—or mistakes them for—the original.

While Colton wrote that "Imitation is the sincerest form of flattery," Oscar Wilde wrote that "Imitation is the sincerest form of flattery mediocrity can pay to greatness." Yet many top-tier impersonators and tribute artists are hardly mediocre. In fact, they often possess talent that equals— or even surpasses, in some cases—those they impersonate. Many have been in show business for years and this is only one facet of their repertoire. Celebrity impersonators often develop a fan base of their own. They openly confess to being "imposters" yet people still clamor for pictures and autographs. Admirers may think this is as close as they will ever get to the original artist.

"There are always going to be more actors than anybody can ever use." —Edward Albee

---

Competition is keen in the world of entertainment and opportunities are often limited, which is true of most creative endeavors. But the idea is to make a living using whatever advantages you may have to make a career, whether in television commercials, feature films or playing superheroes for children's birthday parties. Although playing an imaginary, costumed character for 5-year-olds may not require as much depth of emotion, research or voice control as some other roles or jobs, it does require a certain focus and skill set. It still constitutes being a working actor and portraying someone other than yourself.

ALTER EGOS

Sometimes a tribute artist gets their start because they have heard frequently that they sound "just like so-and-so." So they hone the sound, then work on the look. Others are told they look like someone so often that they study the individual to perfect the appearance, then work on the sound. But to add realism, they have to dig deeper. They must learn the mannerisms, expressions, make-up and more, in order to realistically become that character. If one chooses to follow this path and has no acting experience or training, they must work hard to catch up. How would the character react in different situations? How does the character relate to people in general? How does one come close to the stage presence of the artist they emulate? And of course, you need to know every detail of their lives—because people will ask. Often, even though fans know an entertainer is not the real deal, people often will still talk to the impersonator as though they ARE the real deal, asking about their husband or wife, upcoming movies, recent gossip, etcetera. It's often difficult to separate fantasy from reality and it's the job of a celebrity impersonator to foster the fantasy without overstepping the boundaries of propriety or the law.

Much of this comes from appearance—an image—but as humans, that's what we often base our opinions, behavior and judgements upon. It becomes our reality because appearance is usually the first thing we notice. Drag artists create an entertaining illusion based upon physical appearances. Career coaches offer advice on looking good while job hunting. Casting directors look through photos and send out physical descriptions of what they are looking for in a role. Appearance counts. Normally, an impersonator creates a visual illusion first. But humans are more than their outward appearance and to make it real, other aspects of the personae must be integrated. Tribute artists who sing must deal with another entire aspect of the illusion such as vocal inflections, phrasing, range and delivery of songs associated with their character.

How does one become a top-tier, quality impersonator? It usually starts with the basics; for instance, body type. An individual who weighs 300 lbs, at 5'3" may not present the most believable version of the willowy Cher. Being able to reasonably imitate vocals and speech patterns are a must. Even if no singing is involved, one still has to speak in character. Makeup and costuming, although they can create the miracles seen in drag shows, can only go so far. As with any acting job, becoming familiar with the character is important.

Most impersonators don't have to go to extreme measures to study their character unless they are preparing for a major film role but they do have to prepare. There is a wealth of material from books to videos and films of people in the public eye. Historic figures must do a bit more historical research. It all requires study and analysis. Attention to detail is a must. Does the character part their hair on the left or right side? Does he or she have a slightly nasal tone to their voice or a lisp? Acting classes can help. Learning from and working with experts in hair, costuming and make-up can help. Tribute artists who sing might seek help from a vocal coach and other musicians. There are conventions, books and films about the industry itself.

Theater majors at almost any university are usually required to take classes related to all aspects of the theater. This can include costuming, lighting, make-up, improvisation, voice, stagecraft, playwriting, directing, history and more but it is rare that a student will ever actually apply all of these to any one theatrical endeavor. They may never use some of it at all. There are professional wig masters, lighting grips, prop masters and others who serve the stage normally, but the celebrity impersonator may use all of it, depending on their level of expertise, talent and the venue. They often use every ounce of skill and knowledge they possess, frequently in settings not uniquely suited or built for a production. Again, the musical tribute artist must deal with all aspects of the music and the production, from sound checks and equipment to band members or dancers falling ill.

As with music, sports and other areas, some are truly gifted with a look, natural affinity and often a similar personality to the character(s) they play. They fall into it fairly easily. There are prodigies. For others, it's more difficult. The best performers get "inside the head" of the person they portray and are truly believable. Even when they are playing a character for laughs, there is still a believability factor at work. This is the essence of acting.

"The art of acting is to be other than what you are." —Whoopi Goldberg

---

So how does it feel to try to step into the shoes of some of the greatest public figures and entertainers in history? Does the personae ever carry over into real life? Does the tribute artist see Michael Jackson in the mirror or themselves? Indeed, some people have the foolish notion that impersonators start believing they really are the people they impersonate. Some may feel that the impersonator doesn't have a life of their own. Others may feel they are just trying to cash in on someone else's talent and success.

To do a character justice, any actor must find some part of themselves that can relate to the role. Most develop some empathy for the character they play. An impersonator does tend to identify at least somewhat with the person they impersonate, especially those who portray one individual exclusively. The celebrity they impersonate, becomes like another facet of their own personality. They know the celebrity as well as they know themselves. In fact, it has been reported that when a celebrity passes away, an impersonator often feels as if part of them has died as well or at least a close family member. But death doesn't stop the bookings. Often there will be an increase in requests for appearances after the celebrity has left this world.

But the true professionals are level-headed about the whole business. Julie Myers, who portrays Stevie Nicks, says "It's funny how people automatically assume that you are a super-obsessed fan of the star that you pay tribute to and that you want to be them. Some people also assume that we are out to make a lot of money by using someone else's image and singing their music. I can tell you first hand that is not true. After you have invested in your craft, (costumes, charts, set pieces, instruments, musical equipment, musicians etc…) it can take years to actually make ANY money and one is hardly going to get rich. So why do it? It is mostly for the love of performing and respect for the artist, music or band."

Most people with any talent want to be known and appreciated for their own skills and abilities, not for their presentation or replication of someone else's work. At times, it can feel like cheating if something comes easily or if you happen to look just like someone else. As

Steve Edenbo, who projects a very authentic Thomas Jefferson points out, Imposter Syndrome, with feelings of perceived fraudulence, self-doubt and personal incompetence can be problematic. At some level, all actors know they are not the person they portray. Yet an effective natural lookalike— or any actor—must find a balance and somehow learn to feel comfortable being someone else in their own skin.

In the movie *Coal Miner's Daughter*, Sissy Spacek immersed herself in the role of the very real and very much alive country music legend Loretta Lynn. She stayed with Loretta on and off for a year at her home and on tour, studying her southern speech patterns and singing style. Once Spacek got Lynn down pat, she stayed in character throughout the shoot, even off camera. People visiting the set thought she actually talked that way in real life.

While inflated egos often run rampant in the entertainment world-at-large, as a rule, it doesn't seem quite so prevalent in the realm of the professional celebrity impersonator. It exists, of course. But by and large, there are few traces of exaggerated self-importance, at least outwardly. Perhaps it is because the impersonator must submerge their own personalities in order to seamlessly blend and effectively present the character(s) of those whom they impersonate. There is no room left for inflated egos. It could be that the aforementioned Impostor Syndrome may have something to do with it. Maybe it is because they *are* impersonators and as such, know they are not—and never will be—the original. Even though some of them have perfected the look, sound, movements, choreography and may even have more actual talent than the original, they are still a copy. Some are great copy-cats to be sure, but the vast majority have no trouble remembering that they are *impersonating* another. "It's enough to keep one humble," says a former Willie Nelson impersonator.

Negativity casts a shadow on the ability and artistry necessary to bring to life and channel the contributions of others. It also demeans and overlooks the value of the original. If something is successful, popular and of interest, is it not worth sharing and copying at some level? And does that not require an enormous amount of talent in and of itself? The argument could be made that it is easier to "do your own thing" rather than trying to honestly portray another human being and their work.

PLAYING A ROLE

Maybe the ego gets lost because the sheer work that goes into replicating something that already exists can be humbling. An actor exploring a new role can develop and expand, be original and creative in conjunction with a script. One can bestow a character with unusual vocal inflections, build a backstory that explains an unusual facial tic or twitch, develop a distinctive vocal quality, smoke a cigar, add a prominent limp, scar or facial feature and more. Building a character from scratch requires input from the imagination. But when a character already exists in reality, in many cases the world is already aware of everything there is to know about him or her, thanks to a frenzied media and public obsession with celebrity. It then becomes the job of the impersonator to re-create every nuance to the best of their ability. This requires ongoing dedication, whether the impersonator does one character or many. One can certainly add facets of their own personality, such as their own humor, but it still must fit within the confines of what is already there and what the audience expects.

Award-winning actress and producer Viola Davis once said, "Ultimately, it's not your job, as an actress, to satisfy people's expectations or image of who you should be. Even in your life, you are just who you are." While this may be true in many ways, for the celebrity impersonator, it is *exactly* their job to satisfy people's expectations or image of who you should be. A gifted professional will leave people feeling as though they have met or seen the original.

Actors may draw upon their creativity and imagination to create a unique character. But when the character they play already exists, an actor must draw more upon the discipline of his or her craft to study the person, embody and emulate them in the truest sense of the word.

INTERACTIONS

Human beings draw their own conclusions and make their own assumptions. For the true look-alike or dead-ringer, one who rolls out of bed looking like Johnny Depp or George Clooney, this can bring its own set of problems. It sometimes means interference in their daily lives. People often think nothing of approaching and asking "Do you know who you look like??" (for the millionth time) or "Are you who I think you are…?" There is an underlying thought process that they, like the celebrity they impersonate or resemble, are public property. The public thinks nothing of asking for a photo, not realizing that the person may be distracted, busy or that this is part of how they make their living. Most lookalikes have learned to handle it graciously and are often flattered and even reassured by the comparison and attention. But some dead-ringers have resorted to disguises. Some have admitted that it can get tiring and sympathize with those who are endlessly hounded by paparazzi. If you work at a job where you must engage with the public, it can slow down interactions and transactions. A court reporter, Bettina Williams, who bears an uncanny resemblance to Whoopi Goldberg, is consistently asked for photos in the courtroom.

Almost everyone in this book knows at least one "reluctant lookalike". They may bear a striking resemblance to Chuck Norris, Ellen DeGeneres or another recognizable star, athlete or politician, but they dislike the commotion and play it down. Some will go to great lengths to avoid having the appearance of a public figure. "It can be a nuisance, a pain in the butt," says an anonymous clerk who could pass for a slightly younger Morgan Freeman. A dead-ringer for President Bill Clinton took to wearing unnecessary glasses and growing a beard. A bank teller, tired of the comparisons to Julia Roberts, cut her hair and dyed it blonde.

Most true professionals in the business have embraced their roles and learned to enjoy the experience of being someone else. John Morgan, who impersonates Presidents Bush, Trump and other celebrities, states in the documentary *Just About Famous*, "You have no idea how much fun this is!" Most certainly enjoy the fruits of their labors and indeed, the field can be very lucrative for those who excel at their craft. The best of the best often are paid thousands of dollars per appearance—but they are still far cheaper than the original.

"It must be strange for any celebrity to come face to face with an impersonator. When you're that much of a personal icon and reference point that people impersonate you, it's gotta be a little weird." —Chad Michaels

How do the real stars, the celebrities themselves feel about their copycat counterparts? Many of them realize that it's the tribute artist or impersonator who works hardest to keep the music and the memories alive and well. A good tribute artist can win fans for the original performer, offering more intimate concerts and interactions. Some stars actively promote their "twins." Dolly Parton once had a Dolly Tribute artist join her onstage at Dollywood. Neil Diamond was involved with the filming of *Play Me*, a movie about Neil Diamond tributes. Country artist Tim McGraw has been known to pull a tribute artist up onto the stage with him at a concert, as has pop artist Gwen Stefani. Some use lookalikes as decoys, to deter the press and/or throngs of fans and will offer their blessings, yet others are not so welcoming. Country artist Trace Adkins was involved in a physical altercation with a Trace Adkins tribute artist aboard a cruise ship. To be fair, alcohol was involved.

TRANSFORMING

There are those who feel that if one is not performing Shakespeare onstage in London or appearing on Broadway, one is not a bona-fide actor. Others think that if one plays only certain types of venues or characters or is not immersed in method-type preparation, it is not acting and they are somehow less noble in their pursuit of the art. But Commedia dell'arte was not Elizabethan drama and *Everyman* is not *Cats* or *Two and a Half Men;* yet each had their time, place and function - and each required actors. One is no less an actor because of the setting, venue, purpose or the role itself. A bad actor is a bad actor whether they are playing the part of a real person or playing a rock.

Konstantin Stanislavski, often referred to as the "father of modern acting," first stated that "There are no small parts, only small actors." Before Stanislavski, actors with smaller roles often offered smaller performances meaning that they performed with no depth or commitment, moving around onstage with little purpose. Stanislavski required actors in his productions to commit to their roles completely engaged and inhabiting their character fully. This is exactly what must happen with a high-quality impersonator, lookalike or tribute artist. Luckily, this comes naturally for some people in certain roles. It doesn't mean one is any less an actor because they find it easy to appear as and identify with a part. One does not always have to suffer for the sake of their craft.

"I think of myself as an actor. The duty of an actor is to be able to impersonate anything—a child, an old man, a tree, a chair, a woman." —Barry Humphries

Sometimes an actor who falls into a role easily feels that they aren't pushing themselves to their full potential creatively. This can happen when playing a role or character that is close to one's own looks and personality.

Sarah Mhlanga, a British Meghan Markle impersonator, says this is how she sometimes feels when playing Meghan. "However, some of the jobs, like the dramatization of the Oprah interview for Japanese TV, required me having to re-live Meghan's emotions in order to re-enact that interview realistically. I had to tap into my own emotional work and really embrace all of Meghan's world, feelings, thoughts and experiences. I became her whole character, rather than just imitating her appearance solely."

Kerry O. Ferris, in introducing the paper *Building Characters: The Work of Celebrity Impersonators,* writes that "…celebrity Impersonators inhabit a unique occupational niche: they perform in the roles that other performers are performing. As a result, the work that they do to create and present their celebrity tributes is necessarily distinctive, as is their sense of occupational identity." (The Journal of Popular Culture, Vol. 44, No. 6, 2011, copyright 2011.)

Ferris goes on to state that "…as the practice of impersonation involves the interpretation and replication of the personae of a real individual (either a living celebrity or a historic figure), impersonators have special requirements for the vocal and corporeal execution of their act."

In addition, some impersonators portray fictional characters such as Jack Sparrow, Austin Powers or Disney Princesses. Even so, these characters already exist and the same dedication and meticulous attention to detail is required to make it work.

The professional impersonator, whether portraying an existing celebrity, a figure from the past or a fictional character from a popular movie or book must still undergo a temporary dissolution of most of their own personal identity, have the skill to maintain the character and make the presentation believable. The true professional makes all the difference between a cheap imitation and a polished transformation. And indeed, Kerry writes that "As a result of the special qualities of their professional calling, celebrity impersonators are Masters of Transformation."

"I think impersonation is a great art. It's something that I enjoy doing, in a frivolous and lighthearted way."
—Andrea Riseborough

In spite of some considering it to be imitative and commercial, the art of impersonation is still a valid theatrical endeavor, worthy of pursuing, worthy of an audience and worthy of study. It has been said that inspiration can come from anywhere. The celebrity impersonator usually finds inspiration in the greatness, talent, spirit, humor or music of those they impersonate.

Austin Powers doesn't actually exist. Tickets to Rolling Stones concerts are expensive. Michael Jackson and Elvis are no longer with us. But you *can* see Greg Thompson as Austin Powers, Johnny Moroko as Mick Jagger, Michael Firestone as the King of Pop and a host of entertainers as Elvis. And sometimes that is, to paraphrase a line from a Jack Nicholson film, "…as good as it gets."

Impersonators in the Movies

It has been said that one of the toughest jobs for an actor is to play a real life person such as in the currently popular biopics. When an actor plays a fictional character, they usually have creative license to invent whatever mannerisms, speech patterns, quirks and incidental character traits they see fit.

Actors playing well-known real people have more to draw on in terms of research and documentary evidence but the actor must still tap into the history, motivation, intellect and emotion; they must analyze the body and voice in depth, in order to create authenticity and not simply imitation.

Eddie Redmayne, Jamie Foxx, Sissy Spacek, Jennifer Hudson, Tom Hanks, Anthony Hopkins, Leonardo DiCaprio are just a few acclaimed actors from the long list of those who have portrayed real people in films, from President Abraham Lincoln to country music star Loretta Lynn.

David Oyelowo as Martin Luther King Jr. ('*Selma*')

"David Oyelowo, whose King radiates an authenticity unseen in the biopic form since Daniel Day Lewis (appropriately awarded) "Lincoln." —Indiewire

Meryl Streep as Former Prime Minister Margaret Thatcher ('*The Iron Lady*')

"Stiff legged and slow moving, behind a discreetly applied ton of geriatric makeup, Ms. Streep provides, once again, a technically flawless impersonation that also seems to reveal the inner essence of a well-known person." —N.Y. Times

Daniel Day-Lewis as Christy Brown ('*My Left Foot*')

"By some feat of imagination and empathy, he then made Lincoln seem real. This wasn't just mimicry. It was as much to do with expressing the feelings and thought processes of the President at a pivotal moment in his life as it was with appearance or voice."
—The Independent

SECTION 2
Meet the Cast

Billy Buchanan

as Chuck Berry

as Sam Cooke

as Ray Charles

as Little Richard

BILLY BUCHANAN pays tribute to many of the essential soul, blues, and early rock trailblazers with true authenticity. Born and raised in Cleveland, OH, the city where DJ Alan Freed first coined the phrase "Rock and Roll," Billy has a deep musical heritage that began while he was looking through his father's LP's as a child.

As an award-winning recording artist, Billy released six albums as a solo artist and two albums with two different bands. He's had three Top 20 songs on the CCM charts and has performed in all 50 states and in 26 countries. As a sideman and multi-instrumentalist, he's played bass, guitar, keyboards, or sang background vocals for many great artists, including Grammy winners Rebecca St. James, Michael Tait, and John Carter Cash.

Billy has opened for or shared the stage with Tower of Power, Jersey Boys On Tour, Harry Connick Jr., Betty LaVette, The Four Tops, Morris Day and The Time, Chaka Khan, KC & The Sunshine Band, Funky Meters, Josh Turner, Martha Reeves & The Vandellas, Brothers Osborne, David Ryan Harris, Shawn Mullins, Sixpence None The Richer, JohnnySwim, The New Orleans Suspects, The Atlanta Rhythm Section, Joy Williams (from The Civil Wars), Super Cat, G Love and Special Sauce, 24-7 Spyz, Switchfoot, Extreme, P.O.D, N'Dea Davenport (from The Brand New Heavies), Skillet, Alice In Chains, Rebecca St. James, Salt-n-Pepa, and Jennifer Nettles, from Sugarland, to name a few.

As a songwriter, he's written songs with Dave Cobb, Busbee, Mike Hartnett, Marc Byrd, and other established writers. He was a Top 3 finalist in The PGA Tour Songwriting Competition, a winner of The Atlanta Local Music Award, a winner of The Battle for Florida Award, a Top 3 finalist in the Yamaha Music Showcase (two years in a row), and a Top 5 finalist in Buzz Magazine's Musicians For Homelessness songwriting competition. He was nominated for a Dove Award for his role in the touring production, *Hero, The Rock Opera,* and was nominated for two Sunny Awards at The Sunburst Celebrity Impersonator's Convention.

Even with all of this success, Billy has never forgotten where he came from and the artists that inspired him as a child. To pay tribute to them, the city that he loves and the music that changed his life—and the lives of millions around the world—he created *The Pioneers of Rock 'n Soul Show,* a high-energy celebration paying homage to the sounds of the '50s and '60s.

"It's been a long time coming. But I know a change is gonna come…" —Sam Cooke

21

Carla Del Villaggio
as Barbra Streisand

Photo © Michael Cairns, Wet Orange Studio

THE LEGENDARY BARBRA STREISAND is a hard act to follow. In fact, it would be just a hard act, for most people. Not for Carla Del Villaggio, the classically trained lyric soprano and Professor of Music. She nails it, hands down, from the voice, to the 'look,' to the onstage banter; her show *Simply Streisand* is simply perfect. Like buttah...

Q. How did you get started?

"When I met my 'other half,' Paul Brown, I had recently retired from singing Opera (I have my Master's Degree in Voice with an Opera Specialization). He enjoyed singing karaoke, which I had never done. So I would go with him but the only thing I could think of to sing were Streisand tunes, as I've been a fan all my life. Inevitably someone would approach me saying 'Has anyone ever told you that you look like Barbra Streisand?' Most of my life I had heard that comparison, which I took as a compliment. After hearing these comments over and over, Paul started talking to me about becoming an impersonator or Tribute Artist. I thought he had lost his mind and I fought it for a couple of years. He finally twisted my arm to give it a shot in 2006 at a convention for professional impersonators. It was 'raw' at the time; my look needed work, my voice (impersonation) needed A LOT of work but I received some great feedback and encouragement. So, here we are, many years later and going stronger than ever."

Q. Have you ever met Streisand?

"Unfortunately, I have never had the honor of meeting Ms. Streisand. I have, however, seen her in concert four times - each one a life changing experience and a master class on performance, communication with an audience and interpretation of lyrics. I learn every time I watch or listen to her. I am, however, friends with a couple of her first cousins and her 104-year-old Aunt. They attend my shows whenever possible and have been absolutely lovely and complimentary. That may be the closest I'll ever get to her."

Q. What was your most memorable performance so far?

"In June of 2012, I was asked to perform at the (former) Bon Soir nightclub in NYC. This is where Barbra Streisand made her professional debut. They were renovating it and wanted me to re-open the club, as 'Barbra.' I will never forget the feeling of performing in the same room that was filled by her magnificent voice back in the 1960s. I was also the first and only tribute artist to have ever performed there. Dressed in my copy of her iconic blue sailor dress from her first TV special, *My Name is Barbra*, I was absolutely having the time of my life. That's also where I received my first NYC review from the *New York Post*, who said I was '...the next best thing to seeing Streisand herself.' I'll never forget that experience."

Q. We know you have teamed with other Tribute Artists and lookalikes in order to put together some amazing shows. Can you tell us about these?

"I performed "You Don't Bring Me Flowers" with Jack Berrios as Neil Diamond a few years back, and I teamed up with Gary Llewellyn as a young Robert Redford who appeared as I sang "The Way We Were." I have worked with other Tribute Artists as well on different shows."

Q. What are some of the funniest things that have happened on your journey as 'Barbra?'

"There have been a few over the years. During one sold-out show, I was introducing a song and apparently I went on too long for one gentleman who shouted out 'I didn't pay $7.00 to hear you talk!' One of my first shows, back in 2007 I think, was at a 55+ community. I invited an older gentleman onstage with me to sing "You Don't Bring Me Flowers." He actually had a very nice voice, but he was making faces and kind of 'chewing' something during the whole song. After the show he came up to me and apologized, saying that he had just gotten new dentures and they were about to fall out!!"

"This was an hour of heaven!" —Watermark Magazine

Jed Duvall

as Paul McCartney

BORN ON A TOBACCO FARM in the small town of Croom, Maryland, Jed grew up with music all around him; the hymns at church where Jed sang in the choir, the country songs playing on his father's pickup truck radio while he worked in the fields as well as the Beatles records he 'inherited' from older relatives and played until they were literally worn out. After graduating from high school, Jed joined the Army and while at Ft. Belvoir, VA, he traveled to various army facilities performing as Elvis Presley. Jed's own musical endeavors, however, took back seat to his desire to be a professional actor. Accepted into the prestigious American Academy of Dramatic Arts, Jed graduated in 1986 and worked odd jobs to support himself while making the rounds in New York. But by 1996, after getting married and settling down, he took a break from performing, working as a digital imager in the DC area.

In 2005, after almost a decade out of the spotlight, Jed began to perform as Elvis again in national competitions and festivals. But to his surprise, many people started telling him how much he looked like Paul McCartney—even while Jed was in full Elvis costume, sideburns and black wig. Intrigued, he began a McCartney tribute and was amazed by the double-takes of people when he walked into a room as McCartney.

Jed has combined his musical talent and acting skills as well as his natural appearance to present the quintessential and legendary Sir Paul, including the Hofner 500/1 bass guitar, also known as the violin bass or the 'Beatle bass.' It is, indeed, the same model as McCartney's.

Recently, Jed performed—twice—at the Rock and Roll Hall of Fame in Cleveland, Ohio and also at the farewell party for Mike Elliot, former editor of *Time Magazine* and head of the ONE Campaign, an organization dedicated to ending extreme poverty and preventable disease. Jed was hired by the organizer of the event, Bono from U2 and introduced by the founder of MTV, Tom Freston, who commented "You close your eyes…it's Paul McCartney. You open them…IT'S STILL PAUL McCARTNEY!"

Jed has performed hundreds of live shows with his band, The McCartney Experience, and generously donates his time to various charities, including Night of 100 Elvises, which benefits the Johns Hopkins Children Center, the Children's Miracle Network and many others. "I think each of us has a certain gift, something we're blessed with," Jed says. "But if we don't use it to help out others, even if it's just to put a smile on someone's face, it's wasted. I think about that every time I step out in front of an audience."

"And in the end, the love you take is equal to the love you make" – Paul McCartney, The End

Jamie Pagett
as Walter White

Photo © Lee Nichols

BRYAN CRANSTON IS an award-winning American actor, director, producer, and screenwriter. Although he has appeared in many roles and won accolades for producing and directing different projects, he has been most visible in recent years as the character of Walter White in the American series, *Breaking Bad*.

Walter is a high-school chemistry teacher with terminal lung cancer. He teams up with a former student to manufacture and sell methamphetamine to ensure the well-being of his family after his death. Cranston's work on the series was critically acclaimed and the character of Walter White was forever etched in viewers' consciousness.

Jamie Pagett doesn't sell methamphetamine but he looks amazingly like Walter White—and he has met Bryan Cranston.

"The first time I met Bryan Cranston he said, 'Wow, how long have you looked like that?' I said, 'About 25 years.' He replied, 'So, I am a lookalike of you?' He is a wonderful human being."

Jamie continues, "I have been lucky enough to have travelled to America nine times now with the strange and surreal job of looking like the character of Walter White a.k.a. Heisenberg of the award-winning series, *Breaking Bad*. I was very fortunate to be at the Los Angeles premiere of the film *El Camino*, which serves as a sequel and epilogue to the television series and I found myself sitting with all the legendary actors involved in the project. My trips to the film set in Albuquerque, New Mexico, have been amazing."

Like many others, Jamie works only part-time as a celebrity lookalike and his recognition factor may well depend on the longevity and popularity of the show. This is common with lookalikes who are sometimes thrust into the spotlight when someone they resemble achieves fame, fortune or notoriety. There are those who shun the attention and association however, Jamie has learned a lot and taken it in stride. He has met "… lots of awesome, lifelong friends in the whole lookalike family of entertainers, especially on my trips to America," he says.

"In the UK, where I live, I own an outdoor entertainment company which includes paintball games, laser combat, archery, axe throwing and rifle shooting. It's always amusing when a group of customers realize their shooting instructor is Walter White."

Jamie continues, "My dad's name is actually Walter, and my grandfather's name, too, as was my great-grandfather, so it was obviously meant to be."

"I look like everyone." —Bryan Cranston

Matt Cordell
as Jason Aldean

GEORGIA-BORN, cowboy-hatted Jason Aldean is one of country music's hottest young superstars. Playing some of the biggest stadiums in the country with 19 number one hits and more than 15 million total album sales, his hard-driving, high-energy style is a force to be reckoned with. All seven of his previous LPs have achieved platinum certification or better. He has won or been nominated for numerous awards and honors beginning with the ACM Top New Male Vocalist Award in 2005 to his trifecta; winning Entertainer of the Year in 2016, 2017 and 2018.

Matt Cordell has been singing professionally for more than 20 years, paying tribute to Elvis, Bobby Darin and for the past seven years, Jason Aldean. Jason's success has pushed Matt's act over the edge and it has become his favorite tribute to perform. His show, *Just like Jason* is a rock solid, electrifying tribute to the original and Matt is one of the only tribute artists who does Aldean. His passion for entertaining puts him in high demand for requested performances and he has toured extensively, entertaining crowds from Tennessee to Puerto Rico.

Aldean's drummer is a friend of Matt's and Matt says receiving a text from him when Jason got his 3rd Entertainer of the Year award was a great highlight of his 'Just like Jason' career.

"I don't really think that audiences are that much different. I think that a fan is the same whether you are from here or from Japan - you come to a show because you like the music. I don't really see much of a difference anywhere." - Jason Aldean

31

Steve Weber
as Forrest Gump

"THE MOVIE *FORREST GUMP* begins with a feather floating in the sky. The camera follows the feather past church steeples and buildings. As the feather drops down to street level, it passes cars and pedestrians. Eventually, the feather lands at the foot of Forrest Gump. Forrest reaches down and picks it up."

Steve Weber says, "I believe the feather represents opportunities that come into our lives. Our job is to recognize those opportunities and pick them up. That is one of the themes that runs through the movie *Forrest Gump*. Forrest continues to have good fortune (feathers) arrive in his life at the perfect time. And each time, he picks up that new opportunity and makes the best of it. Almost forty years ago, I had the unusual fortune to be told, 'Hey, you look like the guy from *Bosom Buddies*,' a television sitcom from the 1980s. At that time, the people telling me didn't know the actor's name. I didn't know either the show or the actor. Over the next decade however, I became very familiar with Tom Hanks. People told me I looked like him thousands of times over the next 10 - 12 years. I was holding a feather that didn't seemingly have a purpose."

Then the movie *Forrest Gump* came out in July of 1994. "That year for Halloween I was Forrest Gump. I won the costume contest. In March of 1996, I heard a news story indicating that a new restaurant based on the Forrest Gump movie was opening in Monterey; the Bubba Gump Shrimp Company. The feather had once again shown up in my life and landed at my foot. This time, I knew exactly what to do with the feather: I picked it up! Bubba Gump hired me and I worked for them for 15 years. Together we opened 22 restaurants in the United States and 8 international locations. I was Forrest Gump. Another feather kept showing up in my life. The idea of sharing the life lessons from the movie and the concept of 'Gumption' was something I couldn't get out of my head. The movie had touched, moved, and inspired millions of people worldwide. I knew this because I met those people and they told me."

Steve has spent the last 10 – 12 years speaking to groups about the three principles of 'Gumption;' Mindset, Moxie and Graciousness. "I share with youth and business audiences the three most important life lessons from the movie: opportunity, choice, and journey. As Mama Gump told Forrest on her death bed, 'I happen to believe you make your own luck and you have to do the best with what God gave you.' God gave all of us the talented, Academy-Award winning actor Tom Hanks. He gave me genetic luck with an appearance resembling Tom. The feather landed at my foot. I picked it up. Life is like a box of chocolates . . . you get to choose whatever chocolate you want. You get to choose whatever life you want."

Forrest: What's my destiny, Mama?

Mrs. Gump: You're gonna have to figure that out for yourself.

—From the movie Forrest Gump

33

Camille Terry
as Marilyn Monroe

MARILYN MONROE REMAINS ONE OF THE MOST ICONIC and recognizable stars in history. Her legendary status was not dimmed in the least by her death in 1962. Acclaimed as one of the best professional Marilyn Monroe impersonators on the east coast, award-winning Camille Terry has been performing as Marilyn since 1988. Her three-decade career as a tribute artist of the classic blonde Hollywood goddess all started during her college years with a television appearance on the *Joe Franklin Show*, featuring a Marilyn Monroe look-alike contest. She did not win the contest but people there approached her telling her not give up on impersonating Marilyn. They felt she had similar features and qualities. The next day, the same venue had a Jayne Mansfield look-alike contest which she won!

"So, Joe Franklin interviewed me on his show as the winner along with the girl who won as Marilyn. Go figure! LOL," says Camille.

After that, she made numerous night club and corporate event appearances in the New York City area until she moved to Los Angeles in 1989 to work for Ron Smith Lookalikes for a year. Winning that contest as Jayne inspired her to not limit herself to just impersonating Marilyn. In fact, she appeared on *A Current Affair* her very first week living in California, re-enacting Jayne's tragic car accident. In California she learned more about the tribute artist industry and had many wonderful opportunities to travel nationally and internationally, including a trip to Mexico City for a Spanish-speaking Coca-Cola commercial. Other international gigs included Panama City, Panama for grand openings of hotel casinos and for a fashion magazine, performing with other tribute artists in Canada and a night club appearance in Liverpool, England.

She has been interviewed on the *Geraldo Riviera Talk Show, Entertainment Tonite, The Joan Rivers Show* and created a re-enactment of Marilyn's death for *Hard Copy*, in Los Angeles. Camille also starred in the off- Broadway production, *The Ghost of Marilyn,* a dramatic portrayal of Monroe with a who-done-it plot. The real Marilyn sang happy birthday to President John F. Kennedy at Madison Square Garden in 1962. Camille sang happy birthday to the President of Chanel and the President of Radio City Music Hall with the Rockettes. She also sang it again at the Palm Beach Film Festival at Mar-a-Lago. Camille has modeled both jewelry and clothes actually worn by the real Marilyn Monroe. Her sultry, velvety voice continues to melt the hearts of many Marilyn fans. Camille and her husband, Leon Wasiak, who also impersonates a number of characters, produce a 90-minute show dedicated to Monroe's film career called *Silver Screen Star*, incorporating Camille's quick wit and uncanny impersonation. They run their own production company, Camilleon Impersonators, LLC which offers other high-quality impersonators, shows, props and more.

"This life is what you make it." –Marilyn Monroe

Lawrence Calvin
as Steve Harvey

OVERHEARD IN A WALMART: "Hey honey, honey, hurry! Come over here, quick, quick! Look at this! What the hell is Steve Harvey doing shopping at Walmart?!"

In actuality, it was Steve Harvey look-alike Lawrence Calvin, just doing some shopping.

Steve Harvey is a comedian, author, radio personality and has appeared numerous times on television and in films. His impressive list of awards and honors include a Daytime Emmy Award for Outstanding Game Show Host in 2017 and he has won the Daytime Emmy Award for Outstanding Informative Talk Show Host twice.

Lawrence Calvin, originally from Chicago, studied music and trained vocally under the direction of DDS Chorus Director Ms. Jacquelyn Cossack in Chicago. He also studied under Chicago's iconic funk, soul, rhythm & blues master and recording artist, Frederick Doug Shorts. In his mid-20s, he began to transition somewhat deeper into jazz and began to study under Chicago's iconic jazz master and recording artist, Luba Rashiek.

"I currently entertain as a professional old school entertainer who just happens to look a little like Steve Harvey," says Lawrence. "I sing and perform the classic hits of the 50s, 60s, 70s, and 80s as well as Doo Wop, Beach Music, Motown, Soul, Rhythm & Blues, Jazz, Gospel & Country in a stand-alone show called *Tribute to Legends*.

It is rumored that the real Steve Harvey can sing, has a great sense of rhythm and can play the piano and if he decided to go into music, this is what it might look like. Literally.

"My calling is to help people, to teach people, to share with people, until I die. I can never stop doing that. I can't and I don't want to." —Steve Harvey

Jack Bullard
as Jack Nicholson

J ACK BULLARD IS KNOWN IN THE WORLD OF CELEBRITY IMPERSONATORS as a dead-ringer for the legendary Jack Nicholson, the most nominated male actor in the history of the Academy Awards. Bullard travels the world with his trademark sunglasses and cigar and is the official 'Jack' for the Stanley Hotel in Estes Park, Colorado, the inspiration for Steven King's novel and the subsequent horror film, *The Shining*.

In Las Vegas, sharing the stage at an event with the late Louie Anderson, a popular comedian, Bullard was having trouble opening an envelope containing a winner's name. "Do you need a knife?" asked Louie. "I do my best work with an axe," deadpanned Bullard recalling the 1980 classic in which the implement plays a key role.

Leon Vitale was Director Stanley Kubrick's right-hand man during the making of *The Shining* and other films. Staring hard upon meeting Bullard, he said the likeness was incredible, commenting that the movement, mannerisms and even the voice were unbelievably natural and identical to Nicholson's.

A photo double for the film icon, Bullard offers classic examples of people jumping to conclusions and making their own assumptions. If he doesn't go out of his way to set the record straight, people usually come away believing they have met the real deal. "They can't handle the truth," he grins, referencing one of Nicholson's most famous lines from the movie *A Few Good Men*.

"I'm not who you think I am," he tells an excited convenience store clerk, handing him a business card which clearly states that he is an impersonator. Glancing at the card, momentarily confused, the clerk then winks knowingly, conspiratorially, and says "Oh you just hand those out to people to throw them off, Mr. Nicholson… I love your movies!"

On vacation in the Cayman Islands, the owner of a rum company had a photo taken with Bullard who was visiting George Town with his wife. Busy and preoccupied, he neglected to tell the man that he was not the famous American movie star but a lookalike. Two days later, the local paper printed the photo, reporting that the real Nicholson had been visiting the island.

Celebrities occupy an almost mythical place in the hearts and minds of the general public which carries over to their lookalike counterparts. An excited fan once got close to Bullard and shouted "He even smells like Jack!" Another stared at him in a restaurant saying "Look, he eats, too!" Bullard has been asked to leave Downtown Disney twice and is barred from four casinos in Vegas for causing a ruckus merely by walking through the place. Fans begin to gather, wanting pictures and autographs. Unless he has been hired for the purpose of drawing a crowd or entertaining, businesses sometimes feel that large, uncontrolled groups can be a security risk. On the other hand, some establishments welcome him with open arms, ushering him to the front of any lines, wanting the touch of notoriety and publicity associated with the rich and famous.

One of the things Bullard likes best about his job is that he feels like he gets to play an amazing role, receiving accolades as well as criticism. "It's good to be Jack," he says in that slow, distinctive voice which sounds as natural as he looks. When he opens his mouth to announce

"Heeeere's Johnny!" you don't envision Ed McMahon on the *Tonight Show*, you hear the disturbed voice of a psychotic Jack Torrance from *The Shining*.

Another thing Bullard likes about his job is that he gets to meet so many of the real stars. At a single event in Canada, he met country music royalty; Reba McEntire, Charlie Daniels, Roseanne Cash and others. He has partied with the Lynyrd Skynyrd band, Big & Rich and more. He counts among his friends the history channel's Rick and Kelly Dale of *Rick's Restorations*, Danny Coker – 'The Count'- of *Counting Cars* and Discovery Channel's Mike Brewer of *Wheeler Dealer's*.

Bullard does emcee work, meet & greets, commercials, fairs, special events, parties, grand openings, murder mysteries and more. Impersonators often portray more than one celebrity, sometimes many, especially for comic effect, but Bullard is so much like Nicholson that it might be difficult for others to perceive him as anyone else. Even those who hire him for corporate events aren't sure they haven't hired the real thing once he arrives. How does he feel about constantly being mistaken for the enigmatic movie star? Aside from people following him into restrooms asking for pictures and the same pesky general lack of privacy accorded all celebrities, he will tell you "…it beats the hell out of working."

"Star quality is if you're on stage and a cat walks on and they still watch you." —Jack Nicholson

DON'T YOU KNOW WHO I AM?

Fake Johnny Depp

...celebrity look-alikes ...nybody fooled ...ving it!

LA STORIES

SEEING DOUBLE

In Total Film's new regular, we lift the lid on the real Hollywood, peeking behind the velvet curtain of Tinseltown to find the weird and wonderful. And in a town where imitation is the highest form of flattery, check out the Los Angelenos who have learned to live like stars...

WORDS: HOLLY GRIGG-SPALL
PORTRAITS: JAMES STENSON

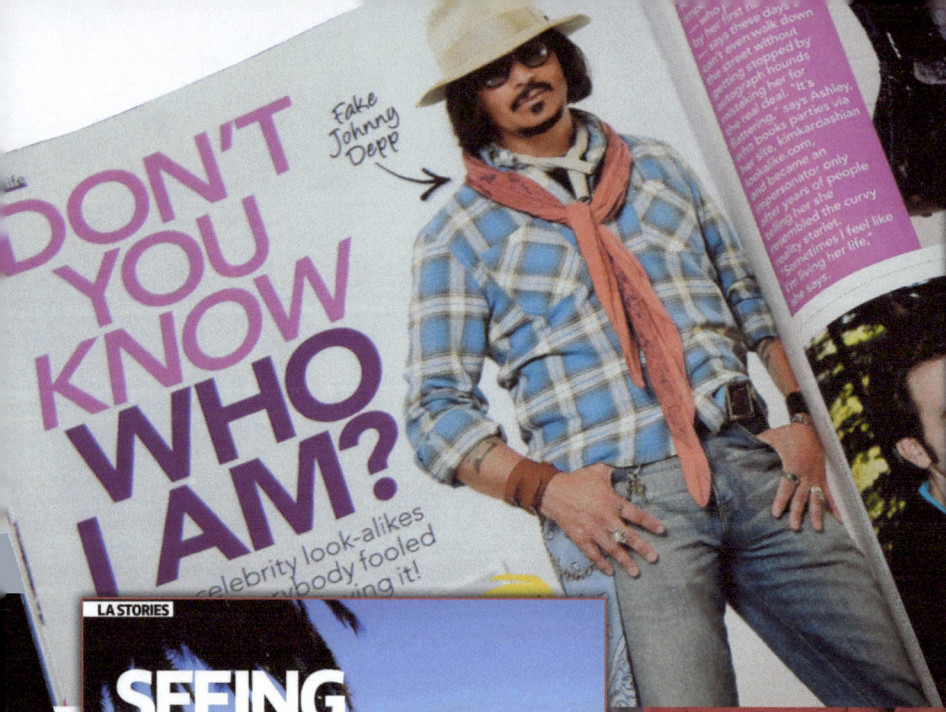

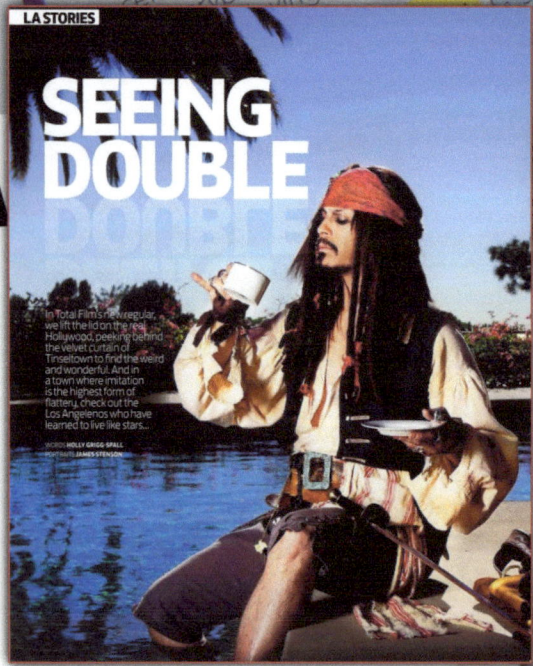

WHO KILLED JOHNN

A Film by Yangzom Brauen

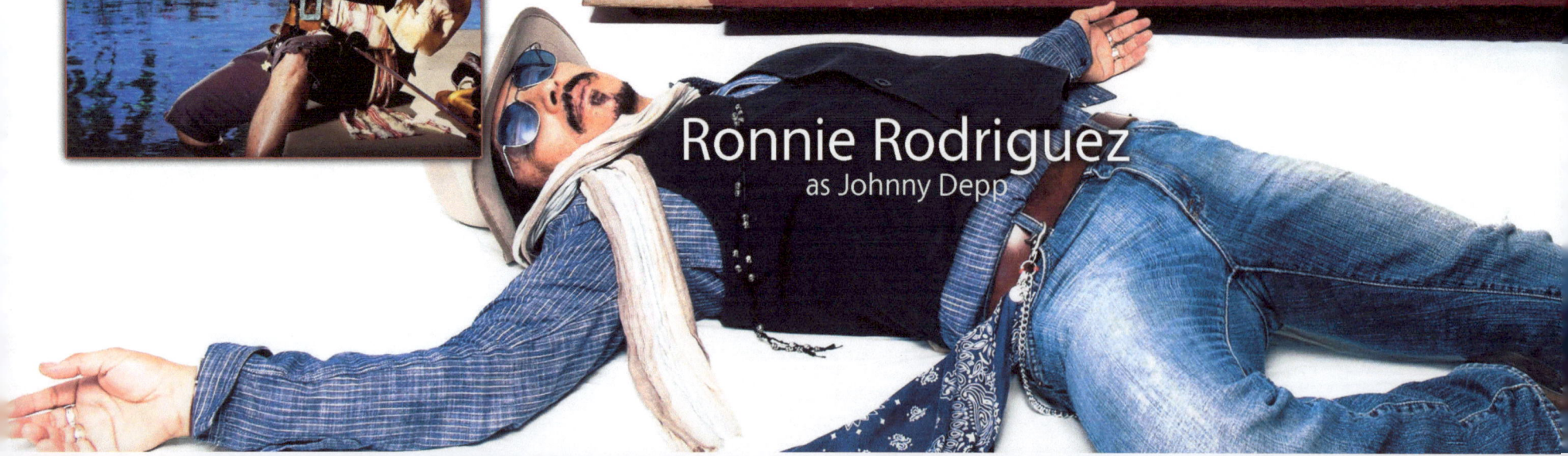

Ronnie Rodriguez
as Johnny Depp

RONNIE RODRIGUEZ IS AN ACTOR AS WELL AS A TOP-RANKED TRIBUTE ARTIST AND HAS APPEARED in various feature films and television shows including, *The Lone Ranger* (2013), *Who Killed Johnny* (2013), *Not Another Celebrity Movie* (2013), *Check it Out!* With Dr. Steve Brule (*Boats*) (2012), *21 Jump Street* (2012) and *Tim and Eric's Billion Dollar Movie* (2012). He was cast as a photo double for Johnny Depp in *Pirates of the Caribbean: On Stranger Tides* (2011), *Jack and Jill* (2011), *Pirates of the Caribbean: At World's End* (2007), *City of Lies* (2018) and *Richard Says Goodbye* (2018).

"This adventure has been not only exciting but very rewarding," he says. Ronnie has appeared on television shows in the United States, Canada, Japan, France as well as Germany. He is also an expert martial artist in Taekwondo and was a nationally ranked 3rd degree black belt. In his spare time, he enjoys playing the guitar, harmonica, and, occasionally, has time to hone his skills in sword fighting!

As a tribute artist, Ronnie is recognized throughout the United States as one of the top-tier, elite performers. Due to his hard work, professionalism and spot-on resemblance to Johnny Depp, he was the honored recipient of a Rising Star award in 2008, Artist You Love to Work With award in 2009, News Hound award in 2010, Best Actor in 2012 and Best Actor in 2016 awards. He is looking forward to future gigs as an actor in feature film, television, and live performances. Says Ronnie, "Now, on to the next adventure!"

He is often asked how it feels to be a lookalike/photo double/stand-in for Johnny Depp? "Well, I usually answer that it feels good!" he says. "But it's intimidating at times, like when I have to read lines to other actors while they deliver theirs. Or when I have to re-enact a scene that Johnny has just done. Or at times being told: '…just do the scene like Johnny would do it!' I remember during a Christmas Special with country artist Carrie Underwood, she came up to me and said, 'This is probably the closest I'll ever get to Johnny Depp. You make me so nervous, I don't know if I'll remember my lines!' I said, 'You're nervous? I'm the one who should be nervous!' She laughed and did her lines just fine!"

When on a set Ronnie often finds himself explaining to other actors and actresses that he's not Johnny. "Even Producer Jerry Bruckhiemer stopped by and said hello to me thinking I was Johnny. I didn't have the heart to say I wasn't! As a look-alike I enjoy the attention and invite questions about how I got started in this crazy business, but really it all goes back to me wanting to be an actor and being told I looked like that guy on *21 Jump Street*. Years later, after playing Johnny's double as Captain Jack Sparrow, I received a call from a couple of producers asking me to come audition for a movie called *21 Jump Street*! It came full circle - I call it Karma!"

"But life inevitably throws us curve balls, unexpected circumstances that remind us to expect the unexpected. I've come to understand these curve balls are the beautiful unfolding of both karma and current." —Carre Otis

Samira
as Tina Turner

© Scott Schmitt

"I WAS TOLD I DANCED LIKE TINA TURNER at a party in 1984 and I wondered who Tina Turner was. I wasn't familiar with the name until a few days later when the video for the song "What's Love Got To Do With It?" was released and I became an instant fan."

Says Samira, "Shortly after, I was at a nightclub that was having a rock star singing contest. I've always loved to sing and dance so I knew I wanted to enter, but didn't know which rock star to emulate. Then I thought of Tina, performed "What's Love Got to do With it?" . . . and won. I was approached by a man who worked for a major Canadian television station. He wanted to put me on the news because Tina was coming to town for her *Private Dancer* tour."

Samira says that Tina isn't known for modesty but more for her in-your-face style and attitude. "Unfortunately, in my Arabic heritage and culture, that's frowned upon so I secretly did the interview hoping my mom would not see it. Unfortunately, I was wrong, so any hopes of pursuing anything in the entertainment field abruptly ended."

In 1992 she met an agent at a disco dance, another passion of hers. "She convinced me to try impersonating Tina again. She got me an interview in a major national newspaper along with other colleagues. I was asked to sit in a chair and by now being a big Tina fan, I figured I would straddle the chair, as she does. BIG mistake, huge embarrassment to my mom and once again I put a career as a tribute artist aside," said Samira.

In 2000 she decided she didn't want to have regrets by not giving something a chance that came so naturally and started again. "I attended my first Celebrity Impersonator Convention in 2003 and another convention in 2004. Since then, I have had some amazing gigs in Australia, Guam & China, to name a few - and a very special one in Nutbush, TN, Tina's hometown. I performed at the local high school to commemorate the opening of a museum dedicated to her." What a huge honor that must have been!

"I am a grown woman and still come up with stories to tell my mom about where I'm going so as not to hurt her. But the public support and reaction to my performance is what keeps me going."

"I believe that if you'll just stand up and go, life will open up for you." —Tina Turner

Photo © Stephen Edgar

Photo © Ido Siman Tov

Photo © Matt Karas

John Di Domenico
as President Donald Trump

Mira Tzur
as Melania Trump

Photo © Matt Karas

EMMY NOMINATED, AWARD-WINNING actor, writer, impersonator and comedian John Di Domenico has worn many hats in his career but none so much as President Donald J. Trump.

"As a kid I had a severe speech impediment. While watching television I discovered I could perform impressions of celebrities; it circumvented the impediment and I could be understood. More important was that instead of being teased about the way I spoke, my impersonations impressed the adults in my life. I grew up in a row home neighborhood outside of Philadelphia and my neighbors would sit out on their steps when the weather was warm. Since I had a captive audience I would do my impressions and they would laugh. Even as a child I found it empowering to be able to make people laugh and smile."

He continues, "In essence, I've been a professional actor, comedian and performer my entire life and I impersonate over 30 celebrities including Austin Powers, Dr. Evil, Dr. Phil, Guy Fieri, Lt. Columbo, Regis Philbin, Jay Leno, Larry king, and many more. The character that changed my life is Donald Trump. I started impersonating Trump back in 2004 and because of that, it put me in incredible position when he announced his presidential run June 2015. Since then I have been interviewed over 300 times by every major news outlet including the *New York Times, Washington Post, NBC news, BBC, ABC Nightline, CBC, FOX News, Politico, The Hill, Huffington Post, CNN* and many, many more. I have traveled all over the world performing as Trump." Plus he has worked on feature films, web-series, commercials, voiceovers, apps, animated series, augmented reality, virtual reality and countless television appearances on *Late Night with Conan, Chelsea Lately, Trumpcast, Today, Fox & Friends, Redeye, This Morning, The Blaze* and many more.

"My proudest moments so far have been winning ABC's *The View's* Best Donald Trump Impersonator competition on national television and the LA Laugh Factory's International Best Trump Impersonator Contest in front of an audience of fellow comedians. Both competitions had the amazing Darrel Hammond on the panel of judges."

People always ask if he has met Trump. "The answer is yes, but I was not in the role of 'Trump' at the time. In the summer of 2000, I performed at Trump's 55th birthday which took place at Trump Marina. I was playing Austin Powers that night. I jumped out of a big birthday cake and joined Trump on the stage to close out the evening."

John has an extraordinary talent for transforming himself into seemingly anyone through the use of make-up, hair and other tools of the trade. What does he think about his rather unusual career?

"What an amazing ride this has been. I often wonder what incredible experience is coming next."

"If you're going to be thinking, you may as well think big." —Donald Trump

W HEN ISRAELI-BORN MODEL AND ACTRESS MIRA TZUR squints her eyes a little and puckers her mouth, suddenly, she's First Lady Melania Trump. Different makeup helps too, of course, but she gets recognized even without it. Ms. Tzur began her career as a ballet and musical theatre performer. She graduated from the prestigious Telma Yalin Arts School with a scholarship provided by the America-Israel Cultural Foundation (AICF) and became a member of the world-renowned Bat Sheva Dance Company.

After completing her Israeli Defense Force military service as a counter intelligence officer, Ms. Tzur moved to NYC where she continued her training at the Lee Strasberg Institute and the Atlantic Theater Acting Company. She has appeared on and off-Broadway, on television, in films and served as artistic director for numerous cabaret dance performances, fashion shoots, fitness commercials and independent film shorts. Behind the scenes, she has served as a producer, writer and founder of two entertainment-based companies.

She began working with Trump impersonator John Di Domenico before the 2020 election, a last minute request of a photographer friend.

"John and I hit it off right away. I had a blast shooting a scene of us directing traffic in NYC and a few days after it was uploaded, the clip went viral on Youtube. As we proceeded to the election, I started to get busier, booking alongside John and alone as Melania's double!" And indeed, they even share the same initials.

"Work hard for what you want in life." —Melania Trump

Photo © Ido Siman Tov

Shannon Michaels
as Bret Michaels

Photo © Bennie Gonzalez

Photo © Cathleen Kulinski Beckwith

BRET MICHAELS, IS AN AMERICAN SONGWRITER, musician, producer, and actor but he is best known as the charismatic lead singer of the rock band Poison.

Shannon Michaels is the ultimate Bret Michaels tribute artist, who not only bears a striking natural resemblance to Bret but combines his realistic look with Bret's persona and vocal capabilities. Shannon has mastered the character of Bret so closely that even Bret Michaels himself stated how impressed he was upon their initial meeting.

Although he does live vocals as Bret, he is especially adept at meet 'n greets and is an experienced and skilled DJ/KJ. Shannon is also a licensed officiant and can perform wedding ceremonies.

Shannon received Rising Star Awards in 2011 in Orlando and in Las Vegas. In 2012, he also received the Congeniality/Richard Hampton Award in Orlando, Florida. He was featured in the documentary film *Almost Famous*, released in 2015.

Shannon appeals to all Bret fans and enthusiasts with the warm, approachable personality, style, and charm that Bret Michaels is famous for and exudes that elusive Rock Star Legend aura. A popular choice for weddings, engagement parties, night clubs, bars, birthdays, anniversaries, tail gate parties, grand openings, and more, he travels nationally throughout the year from his base location of Madison, WI.

"My life is part humor, part roses, part thorns." —Bret Michaels

Terry Lee Goffee
as Johnny Cash

Q.
HOW AND WHEN DID YOU GET INTO THIS BUSINESS?

"I have been a Johnny Cash fan since my father first introduced me to his music when I was about 7 years old. After high school I performed in several local bands and always included a good portion of Cash songs. I continued to be involved in the music business in one form or another for the next thirty years. At some point I began to notice that Tribute Bands were becoming more and more popular. These were mostly Rock 'n Roll bands; Beatles, Doors, Joplin and the like. At the time I wasn't aware of any Johnny Cash Tribute Bands so I decided to put one together in 2002 to see if there was any interest. I am fortunate to have grown to a height of six feet two inches, Johnny's exact height, with similar facial features and a vocal range very close to Johnny's. In short, I just feel like this was something I was meant to do."

Q. Do you do other characters?

"Someone was once quoted as saying "Do one thing and do it well". With that in mind I have put all my focus on being the best Johnny Cash I can be."

Q. You travel on a big tour bus like Cash used to - Got any bus stories?

"Anyone who has traveled regularly in a tour bus will tell you that breakdowns are just part of the deal and we have certainly had our share. One night, we were in Kentucky performing at an after-Derby party for Jerry Bruckheimer, the movie and television producer. On our way out of town we had to climb a fairly steep hill to get back to the highway. We didn't realize the bus was leaking transmission fluid. We made four attempts to get to the top of the hill before we finally made it. There was a little neighborhood bar at the bottom of the hill and a group of about dozen patrons were standing outside cheering for us every time we made another run at the top. Don't know for sure but I think they were making bets on whether or not we were going to make it."

Q. You and your band have traveled overseas. How was that?

"On our first trip to Ireland something went awry with the paperwork. Our passports were confiscated and we were told to return the next morning at which time we were summarily deported back to Newark, NJ and had to sit around the airport for 8 hours while the promoter purchased new airline tickets and worked out the glitch with the paperwork. Fortunately, the tour was a big success and since then we have performed in England, Germany and have completed three more tours of Ireland."

Q. Any negatives to what you do?

"There is never enough time to sing every Johnny Cash song the audience wants to hear."

Q. Have you met any of the Cash family/band/etc?

"We have met a few Cash family members, including Johnny and June's son John Carter as well as Johnny's brother Tommy and his sister Joanne Cash Yates. We have performed several concerts with Joanne. We have also met and performed with Marty Stuart who used to be married to Johnny's daughter Cindy and was part of Johnny's band for a couple years."

Q. I know you work a lot of fairs. What is your favorite venue and why?

"The fairs are great because they are pure Americana. If you want to meet the people that make this country great visit a County Fair. With that said, I also enjoy playing casinos. One of my favorites would be Turning Stone Casino in Verona, NY."

Q. What would you be doing if not this?

"I spent 20 years off and on working in radio, starting as a DJ before moving up to Music Director and finally Program Director. It was a way of staying involved with my passion; music. If for some reason I was no longer able to perform I would go back into radio."

Q. What has been the best part of this ride?

"Definitely the people we've met along the way. Many of them started as fans and have become good friends over the years. A close second would be the towns, cities and countries we've had the opportunity to visit."

"Well, we're doin' mighty fine, I do suppose
In our streak of lightnin' cars and fancy clothes
But just so we're reminded of the ones who are held back
Up front there ought to be a Man In Black."

—Johnny Cash, "Man in Black"

George Kane
as Hugh Hefner

HUGH HEFNER, FOUNDER AND EDITOR-IN-CHIEF OF *Playboy Magazine* and Patron Saint of Playboy bunnies everywhere may have gone to that 'rabbit hutch' in the sky, but his legacy lives on. He has been called a leader in the sexual revolution. His lifestyle embodied high living, sensuality and sophistication. After his death, CNN called him a cultural icon who championed a more libertine view of sexuality that went against the puritanical elements of the times and turned his brand into a forum for sexual freedom and progressive politics, advocating for civil rights and free speech. His legendary parties, exploits and the scantily-clad ladies between the pages of his publications—and often between his sheets—were the stuff adolescent boys dreamed of.

Once a high school principal, George Kane entered a Hugh Hefner lookalike contest at Fantasy Fest in Key West, Florida in 2010 and won. One week later he was hired for a NYE party in Sacramento, California. This was his first gig. Since then, he has appeared at more than 140 events throughout the US, Mexico and the Dominican Republic. His bookings have remained steady even after Hefner's death. "When 'the Hef' makes an appearance," he says, "it results in an awesome time for everyone involved. Every event I go to presents a different vibe. I am just a party animal that loves being with people," says George.

How do people react to seeing him? Does he have any particularly memorable gigs? Recently at an event in Oxford, Mississippi, he was sitting in a VIP booth with two bodyguards so the crowd wouldn't overrun him and two girls crawled under the table to get to him. The week before, he was at the Old Playboy Club in Lake Geneva, Wisconsin—now the Lake Geneva Convention Center—for a gig. Accompanied by a playmate and a bodyguard, they were waiting outside in 5-degree weather for the sound of a helicopter arriving, which was supposed to signal their entrance.

They finally got the cue to enter and the door was locked! They were freezing. Ultimately, they had to go around to another door. Upon entering, George took to the stage and the mic wasn't working. Ah, such are the trials and tribulations of the rich and famous! George says life lessons he has learned from playing Hefner are;

1. Be classy and accept everyone you meet.

2. Always say something nice to everyone and make them feel important - which they are.

"I would like to think that I will be remembered as someone who had some positive impact on the sociosexual values of his time. And I think I'm secure and happy in that." —Hugh Hefner

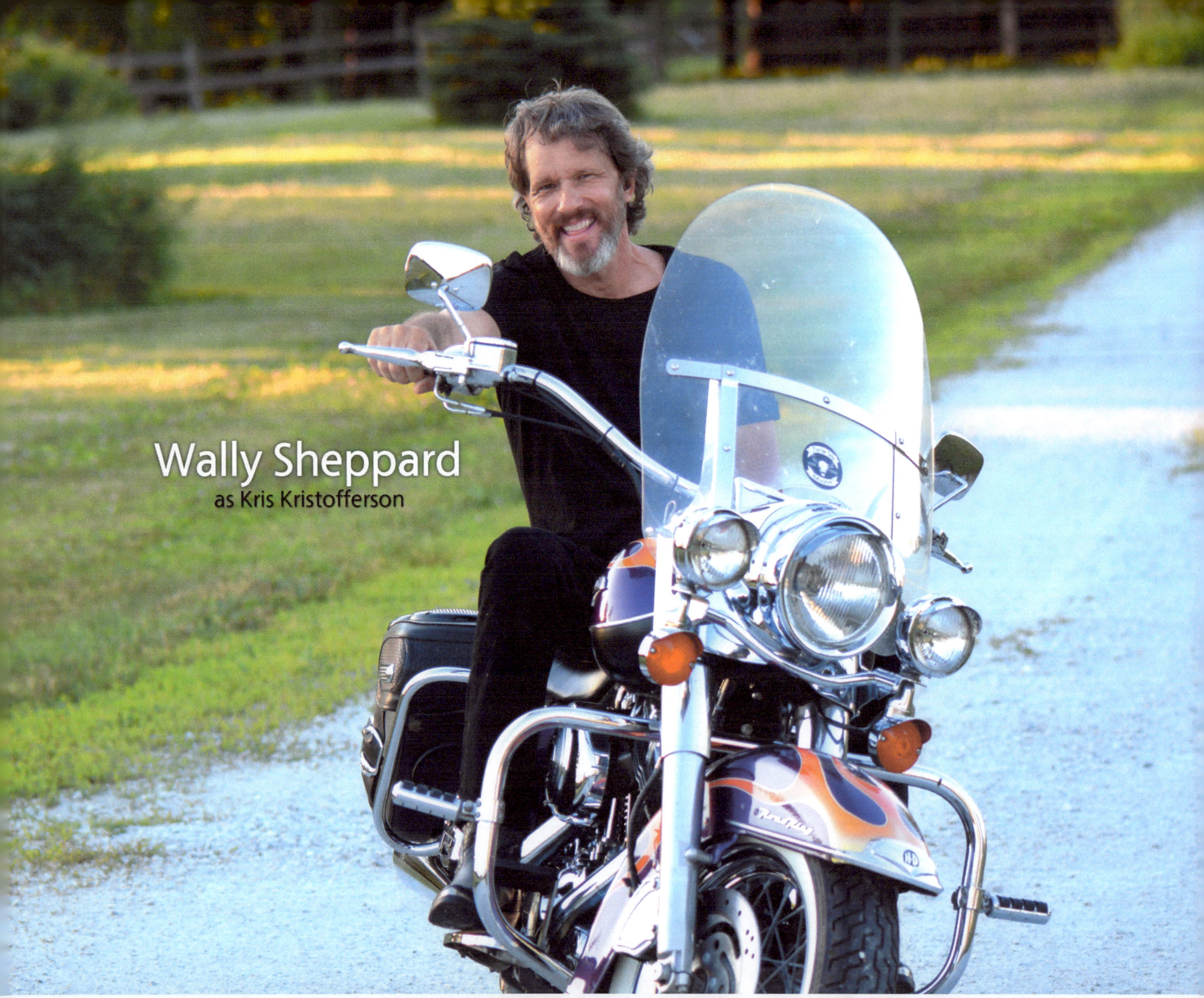

Wally Sheppard
as Kris Kristofferson

TEXAS-BORN KRIS KRISTOFFERSON wears many hats. He is a singer, musician, and actor. A military brat as a kid, he later attained the rank of Captain in the Army. He has been a helicopter pilot, a Golden Globe award winner and a Rhodes Scholar but his biggest successes have come from the songs he's written throughout the years, which include the classic "Me and Bobby McGee" and "Help Me Make it Through the Night." His collaboration in 1985 with Johnny Cash, Willie Nelson and Waylon Jennings in the supergroup The Highwaymen and their affiliation with the outlaw movement helped change the face of country music and Nashville forever. He has a variety of film credits to his name and won a Golden Globe award for the movie *A Star is Born* with Barbra Streisand. In 2012, he appeared in *Joyful Noise* with longtime friend Dolly Parton. In his early days, struggling as a songwriter, it is said that he once landed a helicopter on Johnny Cash's lawn to get his attention. It must have worked because later Johnny recorded "Sunday Mornin' Coming Down" and Kris Kristofferson won Songwriter of the Year at the Country Music Awards. Wally Sheppard is a dead-ringer for Kristofferson, but he doesn't fly helicopters.

Q. When did you first become aware of the resemblance?

"I remember the first time I saw Kris, I was still in grade school and the movie *Convoy* made its television debut. Kris portrayed the 'Rubber Duck,' wheeling a tough-looking Mack truck pulling a tanker trailer. It made an impact on my impressionable young mind. During a commercial break I asked my mother about the lead character and who he was. She said he was a singer and a song writer that also did some acting. At the time, I never imagined that years later I would be hearing how I looked like him from total strangers, even being stopped for my autograph or picture. The first time I heard it was at a party. I was in my mid 20s; 'Do people tell you that you look like Kris Kristofferson?' asked a stranger. Since then I can't count how many times I've been asked that same question."

Q. How have you prepared, as a Tribute artist?

"In recent years, I've realized life is short, so I decided to do something with this resemblance. I began to investigate the lookalike/impersonator industry. I have studied Kris's huge volume of work, songs, videos and movies. I began learning guitar and practiced singing his songs. The more I studied him the greater my respect for him grew."

Q. Have you ever met him?

"I've seen him in concert several times. I even caused a bit of a stir in the audience. But my real mission was to meet him. I made my way to his tour bus. His crew was busy loading up guitars, they spotted me and started calling me Kris but as it turned out, he was done for the night and was not meeting fans. One of the guys took it upon himself to get me an autograph. He returned with a signed cd for me. It was as close as I was going to get. I left smiling and happy, maybe next time."

"Nothing ain't worth nothing but it's free." —Kris Kristofferson, Me and Bobby McGhee

David Born
as Robin Williams

Photo © David Born

D AVID BORN RECENTLY STARRED IN THE DOCUMENTARY, *The Price of Fame: Robin Williams* on The Reels Channel and has appeared on numerous other TV shows, reality and game shows as Robin including *The Next Best Thing*, *Family Feud Celebrity Look-a-Like-week*, *Community* on NBC, *Last Comic Standing* and *Tim & Eric's Awesome Show*. As an actor, David has appeared in over 60 movies and television shows.

Q. How did this all come about?

"In 1978, I was a 'theater guy' with long hair, high energy and did a million voices. I went to a McDonalds, ordered and when pulling up to the window, I dropped my change. When I made a funny, offhand remark, the girl at the window screamed at the top of her lungs 'Ahhhh! It's Mork! It's Mork!—wait a minute, you ain't Mork . . . you look just like Mork. . . !' But I had never seen the show *Mork & Mindy* and had no idea who Mork from Ork was! It's now part of show business history that the popular television show helped to propel the late Robin Williams to the superstardom he well deserved. And as soon as the show came out, I began getting the comparisons."

Q. What sort of comparisons?

"They compared our high energy personalities and the look. Then I saw 2 of his movies and realized they were right; Robin and I were identical. What a weird feeling! I did not watch his movies or comedy shows for the next 10 years. I refused to. I felt that I had to find myself first as an artist. During this time people still kept saying, 'You're just like Robin, you must worship him!' I would reply that I had not seen his work. It was a curse in the beginning, then, over the next 20 years, it slowly evolved into a blessing."

Q. Have you ever met Robin?

"I'm a career stage, film and television actor and member of SAG-AFTRA and AEA. For 10 years I was the Groucho Marx of Texas appearing over 150 times at events. I am also a seasoned Lt. Columbo impersonator although that is mostly for murder mysteries these days. I've done a hundred plays and tons of TV, film and commercial work, yet I was 'discovered' as Robin. I started doing the impression in 1990 at age 30, but did not take it seriously until I hit 40. As I aged, I looked more and more like him. We actually met in 2002 after a show in Houston. We spoke in depth about my comparison to him, the impression, struggles and all the work I had done . . . both as an actor and an impressionist. Robin was very supportive and generous. At the end of our conversation he said, 'Well David, I have a lot of movies and projects coming out in the next year and if anything I am doing is helping you to get more work, go get 'em, boss!' We then took a photo. I was 42. Robin's 9 years older than me. Now at age 57, I look just like Robin in that photo."

Q. How do people react to you as Robin?

"I have been mobbed on Hollywood Boulevard and had people cry because they were so excited. A live auction event was shut down and I had to be chauffeured off site after my performance because so many thought I was really him."

Q. What other Hollywood stars have you met?

I have met many but I was recently working with Woody Harrelson on a big movie called *The Highwaymen*. He watched *The Price of Fame: Robin Williams,* then invited me to his bus to talk about it.

Q. What are some of the advantages of being Robin?

Once going into Canada, I was asked to go to the customs line for further questions. It was odd. I had just been to Canada, but this was now after 9-11. As I stood there in a very long line, I just knew I was going to miss my performance that evening. The agent was circling the airport waiting for me. Then—a lucky break—a Canadian customs officer looked at me and said: 'Mr. Williams?' I turned toward him, in full costume, of course, and just looked at him. He said, 'What are you doing in this line?' I said, 'I had the same question, Chief.' He took my ID and passport, came back and said, 'You're good to go.' Ahh...celebrity life."

Q. What's the best thing about this celebrity life?

I met my hero . . . and he was simply the best. I will always honor his life and try to bring awareness to Lewy Body Dementia, a progressive degenerative disease of the brain. It shares symptoms, and sometimes overlaps, with several diseases, especially Alzheimer's and Parkinson's. Lewy Body is terminal with a 3 – 5-year survival rate. Robin contracted Lewy Body along with Parkinson's and was fighting for his life; he lasted 3 years. My goal thru a tribute is to make sure people understand both why we lost Robin . . . and why we loved him so much."

"The human spirit is more powerful than any drug and that is what needs to be nourished: with work, play, friendship, family. These are the things that matter." —Robin Williams

Natalie Black
as Adele

NATALIE BLACK IS THE UK's number 1 choice when it comes to booking an Adele tribute act and she has now performed in countries around the world, including Greece, Tenerife, Italy, Netherlands, Latvia, Egypt, Turkey, Malta, Cyprus, Portugal, Germany and even as far as Dubai plus a nationwide tour in the UK. She began her singing career in 2004, singing cover songs locally in bars and restaurants. Natalie began performing as Adele in 2011 and leaves audiences spellbound with her rich and soulful voice, replica costumes, and a natural likeness. Her act can include up to a 90-minute concert which has been booked for many prestigious events, including private celebrity parties, weddings, festivals and even the Queen of the UK at a Royal Ascot event. She describes her transition into performing a tribute to Adele as a calling.

Q. What do you mean by a 'calling?'

"Something just came to me one day and told me to do it, I just believed in myself and I thought of nothing else for an entire year while I focused on creating the new me."

Q. How has doing this affected your life?

"It's benefitted my life in so many ways, and my children's. I never imagined I'd work abroad with my singing. I've also been very fortunate to be able to buy a beautiful family home from my earnings to raise my kids in. I'm very fortunate and I'm very grateful for everything."

Q. Are there any negatives to being in this business?

"It's not easy money. It does mean most weekends are spent away from my children and husband travelling for hours to shows and lots of hotel rooms! One time I was travelling to Greece (Crete) for a show in a very posh hotel and my suitcase didn't arrive on the carousel at the airport. I was told it wasn't going to get there in time for my show and the only clothes I had were the ones I was wearing! I had to borrow absolutely everything from cast members at the hotel! Luckily someone had a dress in a sort of similar size to me. The shoes though, were hideous, but I got though the show and tried to remain professional, smiling on the outside - but inside I was cringing and dying! It felt especially weird not to have my eyelashes on which are a ritual and a must for every show!

Q. Any other crazy gigs?

"Once I was performing a show at a casino, my husband was with me for the evening and in charge of lighting and the smoke machine—he was very keen on the smoke machine, to the point I had to ask him to stop pressing the button because I could barely see the audience in front of me! I'd just finished my last song and was about to perform my encore when all of a sudden the fire alarms went off! Que evacuation of 2 floors of gamblers until the fire brigade gave the all clear! I said, "I'm sorry, it's a mistake. It's my smoke machine, it's not a real fire." But they said certain procedures had to be followed, so about 300 people stood outside in the cold giving me the evil eye! The casino lost thousands as we were outside a good 2 hours before the fire brigade did their thing. I still got paid though, hey ho."

"I wanted to be a singer forever. But it's not really my cup of tea…. having the whole world know who you are." —Adele

Photo © Justin McKee

C.J. Morgan
as Dolly Parton

THE FIRST THING DOLLY PARTON said upon meeting C.J. was "Lawd, we could be sisters!" And indeed, even without the big wigs, make-up and over-the-top sparkles there is a definite resemblance. "Their bubbly personalities, voices and values are very similar," notes a friend. "C.J. doesn't really have to try very hard to be Dolly."

As a musician, actress and BMI-affiliated songwriter, C.J. has traveled and performed across the country, appeared on television, stage and in films, served two internships at Sundance Film Festival, wrote, produced and directed a children's musical, studied improvisation for five years, played keyboards and sang back-up for a number of touring bands and more. She plays 5 instruments, has two college degrees, an extensive background in corporate training and is a published author. She can impersonate other characters but says Dolly is the easiest, most requested and closest to her heart. She began impersonating Parton in 2011 when friends asked her to pose as the buxom, blonde country songbird to help publicize their new business. These friends knew the real Dolly well and through them, C.J. was able to meet the star in person on several occasions. She says "Dolly is just as gracious, genuine and beautiful as you would expect. I was so tongue-tied I could barely speak because she was one of my genuine heroes and one of the reasons I got into the music business in the first place. Dolly's music got me through some of my darkest times."

With deep roots in East Tennessee and strong family ties to the area, C.J. has lived there much of her life. It is also an area where tourists might be on the lookout for the REAL 9 to 5 gal as Ms. Parton is also from the area. But indeed, even a faux country queen can be a distraction. How do people react to C.J. as Dolly? "When I lived in Nashville, I was always getting comments about being related to her even when I wasn't 'dollied-up.' People would ask if I was her sister. They would do double-takes on the street and in stores. Recently, I was walking along a sidewalk to a gig - as Dolly - and became aware that a car was moving slowly along the street with me. I glanced over to see a cell phone camera pointed my way just as they accidentally bumped into another vehicle."

She continues, "Folks get excited when I wave or pass through a restaurant. Teen-age girls follow me into the restroom and pretend to wash their hands as they scrutinize me in the mirror, wondering if it's really HER! Sitting in traffic at a stoplight, a carload of people next to me rolled down their windows in 30-degree weather screaming "…Dolly! Dolly!…" as if Dolly would actually be driving an old, dirty, beat-up mini-van."

Morgan says she has to go through a short process in order to really look like Dolly, adding the wigs and make-up – but she points out that the real Dolly does too. "She doesn't just wake up in the morning looking like that and neither do I," says C.J. "The blond wigs, beauty mark, flashy clothes and music have all become a part of my alter-ego as well as tools of my trade. One of Dolly's most often- quoted lines is 'It costs a lot to look this cheap,' and I can indeed vouch for that."

Primarily hired for meet and greets, corporate functions, parties and other special appearances, C.J. likes to incorporate some of Ms. Parton's rags-to-riches story and humor into her presentation. "Her story is partly my heritage as well. With a lifelong love of the mountains and the mountain people, I can relate to her in a very authentic way."

69

Indeed, the two women have a mutual interest in education and literacy. C.J. enjoys telling audiences about Parton's philanthropic Imagination Library, a program designed to inspire a love of reading in children. The organization sends free, specially selected, age-appropriate books each month to registered children from birth to age 5. "Dolly's father and my own father grew up in a time and a place where education and learning weren't as important as the immediate need to put food on the table," says C.J. "They never had the chance to go where books and your imagination could take you. This program can help with reading skills, encourage dreams and more."

Another thing that C.J. enjoys is performing for those who may not be very familiar with Dolly Parton or her music. She says she has won over a few new fans and truly enjoys inspiring others through Dolly's story and music, the way Dolly inspired her.

"I was so desperate to perform that on more than one occasion I sang for the chickens and the pigs and ducks. They didn't applaud much, but with the aid of a little corn, they could be counted on to hang around for a while." —Dolly Parton

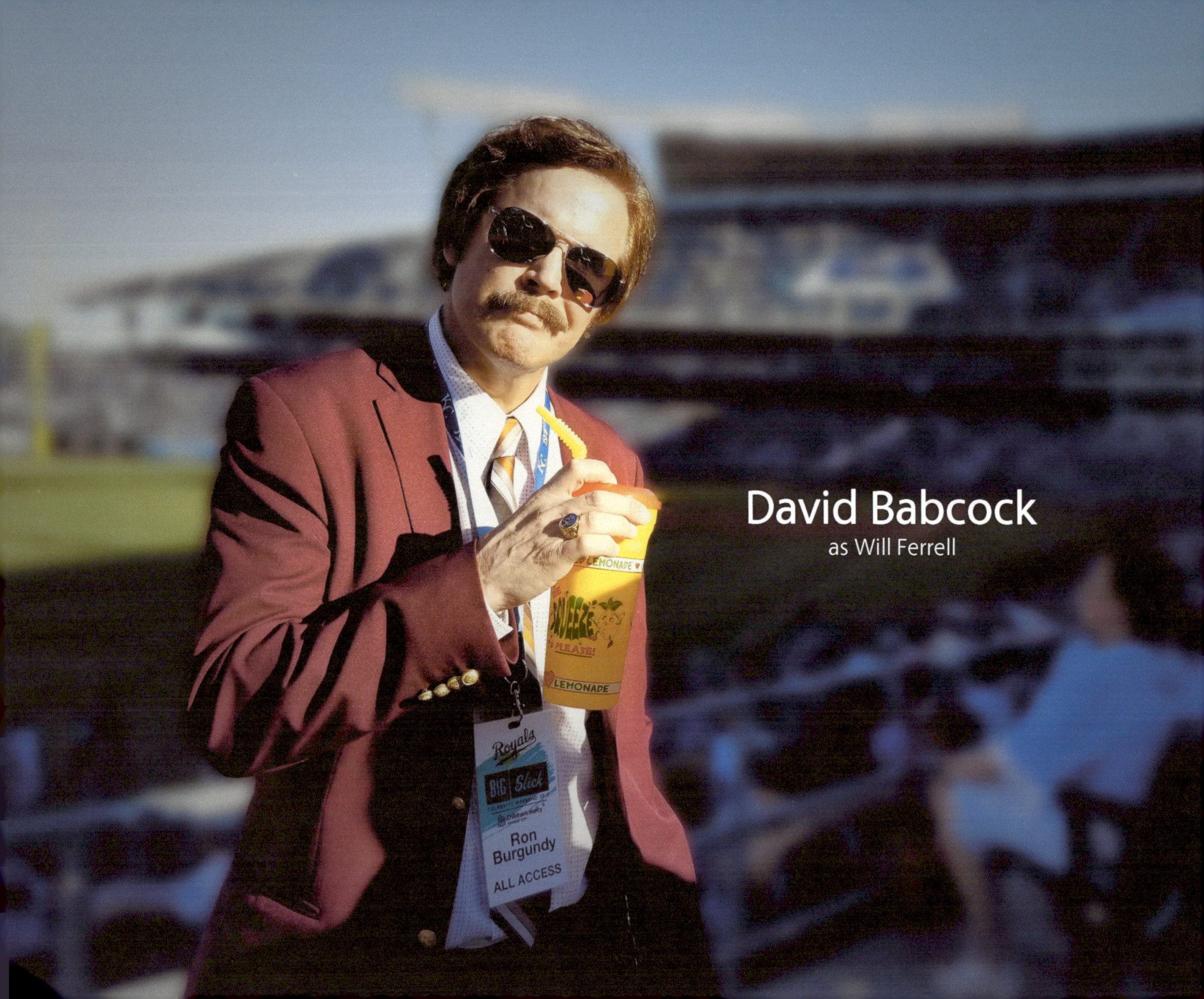

David Babcock
as Will Ferrell

D AVID BABCOCK TRAVELED 25,000 miles across the country in 2017 as award-winning comedic actor Will Ferrell. Or rather, he traveled as characters Ferrell has created on television and in movies such as newscaster Ron Burgundy, race car driver Ricky Bobby and a certain Elf. In effect, like others who portray fictional characters already created and brought to life by someone else, David performs dual roles at one time; he plays Will Ferrell, who plays the aforementioned characters. Although often conceived in the mind of a script writer, these characters are 'born' with the mannerisms, characteristics and look of the actor who made them famous. Such is the challenge of a grown-up man playing an actor who plays an elf.

So how did all this start for Babcock?

"It all started when my stepdaughter invited me and my wife to show up in costume to one of her gigs. She's a singer songwriter. A local radio station was having a costume contest and they were giving away a trip to New York City. She said that since I looked sort of like Will Ferrell that I should come as a Ferrell character - probably Ron Burgundy, the anchorman. I said "No thanks. I haven't worn a costume since I was 12!"

But his wife and stepdaughter continued to encourage him. "I finally went to the thrift store, bought a pair of red pants off the women's rack and an old jacket off the men's rack, spray painted it red and made a microphone out of an old paint roller and some black tape. When I got to the show, I pretended to interview everyone and at the end of the evening everyone I'd spoken with clapped for me. We won the trip. After winning many other contests over the next few years, I was in a bar carrying out a big TV I had won and the manager asked if I would consider hosting their New Year's Eve event in character. He offered me quite a bit of money and a bar tab. I looked at my wife and said 'Baby, we're in business!' So I built a couple of websites and did some social media stuff and things just sort of took off."

"Don't act like you're not impressed." —Ron Burgundy, Anchorman

73

Gregg
Williams
as Clint Eastwood

G REGG WILLIAMS GREW UP ON WESTERNS – especially Clint Eastwood westerns, not realizing he would grow up to *be* 'Clint,' so to speak. He is also one of the lucky ones who has gotten to meet the celebrity he portrays.

Q. So how did you get started in this business?

"Around the age of 25, I cut my hair and started wearing it like Clint. When I added the 'squint' people said "Oh my gosh! You look like Clint Eastwood!" Around 1992 I was at a Macy's fashion show and Diana Dawn, one of the first and best Marilyn Monroe look-alikes was working the event. She was going person to person with a tray of chocolate kisses saying 'Would you like a kiss?' When she got to me, she said 'You could be my 'Clint.' She had a Lookalike business/agency and did not have a 'Clint Eastwood' yet. One week later, there I was at a huge event in Silicon Valley with impersonators of Marilyn, Elvis, Madonna and Cher. I was so nervous I was shaking, but when we entered and someone whistled the 'Clint' theme, from *The Good, the Bad and the Ugly*, the nervousness left me and IT WAS ON !!"

Q. You have a rather unusual presentation, often involving audience participation. Can you tell us about that?

"When I started doing my impersonation of Mr. Eastwood I wanted to bring as much drama and thrills to the tribute as possible. I have friends who are veterans and they helped me to get good at quick-drawing western style, six -shooters, with blanks, of course. People like the thrill of the bang, the smoke and the realism of a face-to-face challenge - and the chance to go against their boss at company parties! I also sometimes take a bullwhip."

Q. You have had the opportunity to meet the real Mr. Eastwood. How did that come about?

"I lived in San Jose many years and have an agent in Monterey. Mr. Eastwood lives in Carmel-By-the-Sea, just south of Monterey. San Jose is a little over an hour North of Carmel. About every 2 weeks I drove south to Carmel to Mission Ranch, a restaurant and piano bar owned by Mr. Eastwood. I was always told that I had just missed him but I still kept going down there. One day my mother, my brother and his family came from Orlando to visit. So I took them down there. I told them that I had been there many times and had never run into Mr. Eastwood, so they shouldn't expect to see him, but my brother Lee said 'He will be there. I feel it…' and he was! That night he came in and sat at the bar. My family was thrilled and when I saw an opening, I approached him. He nodded, indicating for me to sit down."

Gregg told Clint that he had been impersonating him for 20 years and just wanted to get his permission. "He smiled and said 'I've seen your card through John Kelly (my agent in Monterey).' So we chatted. He was very easy to talk to and suddenly I realized that I was talking to him in my 'Clint voice.' He didn't seem to notice, but his pal sitting next to him did and was grinning from ear to ear!! We talked for a while and I gave him my card. He said 'Nice photo,' so I asked him if he had a card. He smiled and said 'I'm not working right now.' At this point his pal laughed out loud."

Q. Didn't you do some work for him?

"He hired me to fill in for him when he was going to be late for his friend's birthday party and another time when a group, the Under 30 Billionaires Club had rented a hall at Tehama, his private golf course and wanted me to entertain. I had them cracking my bull whip and having some fun, then the dinner bell rang and we all went inside to dine. They all sat down so I moved over by the orchestra where they were playing 'Clint' music and started to pack up. Just then a woman said 'Come with me.' So we walked into a back room and there was Mr. Eastwood and a few friends. He said 'Didn't they ask you to sit down and have dinner with them?' I said 'No, I don't think they're the invitin' kind,' realizing that I was again talking in my 'Clint voice.' He said 'Yeah, that doesn't surprise me, I think they're some kind of cult.' So, as we continued to talk, with me still in my 'Clint voice,' his friends were starting to laugh."

Gregg said at that point, Clint's friend/bodyguard decided to give him a bit of a hard time. "So what, exactly do you do?" he asked.

"I said, 'Well when people come to town lookin' for him (pointing to Mr. Eastwood) and they can't get him, I give them the next best thing!'"

He tried again to get to Gregg by saying "So, is that even the right outfit?"

"I said, still in my 'Clint voice,' 'Why don't you ask him, he's sittin' right there.' By then everyone was laughing their butts off and he was red-faced and silent. I also worked at Tehama for a Make-a-Wish fund raiser at which Clint (by now he told me to call him Clint) tried to fix me up with someone. He came up to me and said 'You should go talk to her… (pointing at a woman standing alone) She's a billionaire!'"

"I tried being reasonable, but I didn't like it." —Clint Eastwood

Johnny D. Miller
as The Colonel

A CCORDING TO JOHNNY D. MILLER, Kentucky Fried Chicken's Colonel Sanders is listed as one of the most famous and recognized celebrities of all time. In 1976 Jesus came in first place, Mohammad Ali in second, and the Colonel was 3rd, according to a world-wide survey done back then. Miller probably bears little resemblance to Jesus and even less to Mohammad Ali, but he sure looks a lot like the Colonel! So, how does one get to be a trademarked corporate entity?

"I had been downsized and basically homeless when I was discovered back in the beginning. In 2009 I was approached by Corporate KFC in Louisville and started out as a walking billboard in Yuma, AZ. I hired an agent from Las Vegas who took me under her wing. She sent my entertainment resume to KFC headquarters in 2010," said Johnny.

"In 2011, after one of their other official actors had died, I was the very first person to portray Colonel Sanders as a live actor in a TV commercial after the original Colonel passed in 1980. So far, I have starred in 8 TV commercials and have been to 6 continents, traveling for the brand. I do have permission from KFC to do private gigs but with several restrictions I must follow because my character is trademarked. For example, I am not allowed to go into several other restaurant chains in character."

He continues, "When I travel overseas for the brand I am assigned body guards to protect the Trademark. As the official spokesperson, if something were to happen to me while on an official event, it could affect our company's value on the stock market."

What does Miller have to do to prepare for this role? Is the white goatee and hair real? "As for me, everything is real; hair, facial hair, and tummy full of chicken. I own 8 white suits and have genuine vintage KFC props I own and use for my events. I wear real gold and diamonds. Nothing is fake. I personally own about $7000 worth of authentic KFC memorabilia that I use for my work. It takes me about an hour and a half to get ready for a gig."

Miller seems genuinely fond of the character he plays. "I also have things which belonged to the late Colonel Sanders which the Sanders family sold to me. They endorse and approve of my portrayal, as I do the Colonel with integrity and dignity. KFC likes my work as it does sell chicken for them. I am also a real Kentucky Colonel - a member of the Honorable Order of Kentucky Colonels founded in 1813."

Any downsides to being the face of one of the largest Fried Chicken empires on earth?? "The public always asks me for free chicken - 1000 times a day!!!"

"If I hadn't started painting, I would have raised chickens." —Grandma Moses

AWARD-WINNING TRIBUTE ARTIST BETTY ATCHISON was a singer, dancer, choreographer and stunt performer for Walt Disney World and Universal Studios in Florida for many years. She is now one of the most honored and sought-after Tribute Artists in the nation.

Betty is not only a blockbuster performer, but a gifted costume designer, dancer and make-up artist. She combines all of her talents to present absolutely stunning portrayals of all four decades of Cher and now Lady Gaga, sometimes using a full dance troupe. She recreates, down to the last detail, the intricate costumes, choreography, look and sound of these two powerhouse superstars. Betty has traveled the world offering her high-energy, world-class productions, including Guantanamo Bay, Cuba, entertaining our troops for their Holiday party. It's hard to believe that this glamorous, multi-talented woman has also appeared as the slightly addled Phoebe, from the TV sitcom 'Friends' as well as Ernestine, the irreverent telephone operator character made famous by the versatile Lily Tomlin.

Highly authentic, Betty is a realistic body-double for Cher at a slender 5'8" tall. She uses her own natural waist-length black hair for '70s era Cher appearances and vigorously maintains Cher's trademark 110 lb. physique with a full-time personal trainer. Betty can even offer Lady Gaga's signature 'sparkler bra' to performances when requested.

She devotes a great deal of time and energy to perfecting the skills that have put her on top as one of the look-alike industry's ultimate tribute artists. A favorite among her peers, she is friendly, gracious, professional and has been a mentor and friend to newcomers just starting out in the business.

Betty's advice; "Be honest with yourself assessing what you want to do and what you are good at. Then don't settle for anything less than the best you can be. You can make it happen!"

"Some guy said to me: Don't you think you're too old to sing rock n' roll? I said: You'd better check with Mick Jagger." —Cher

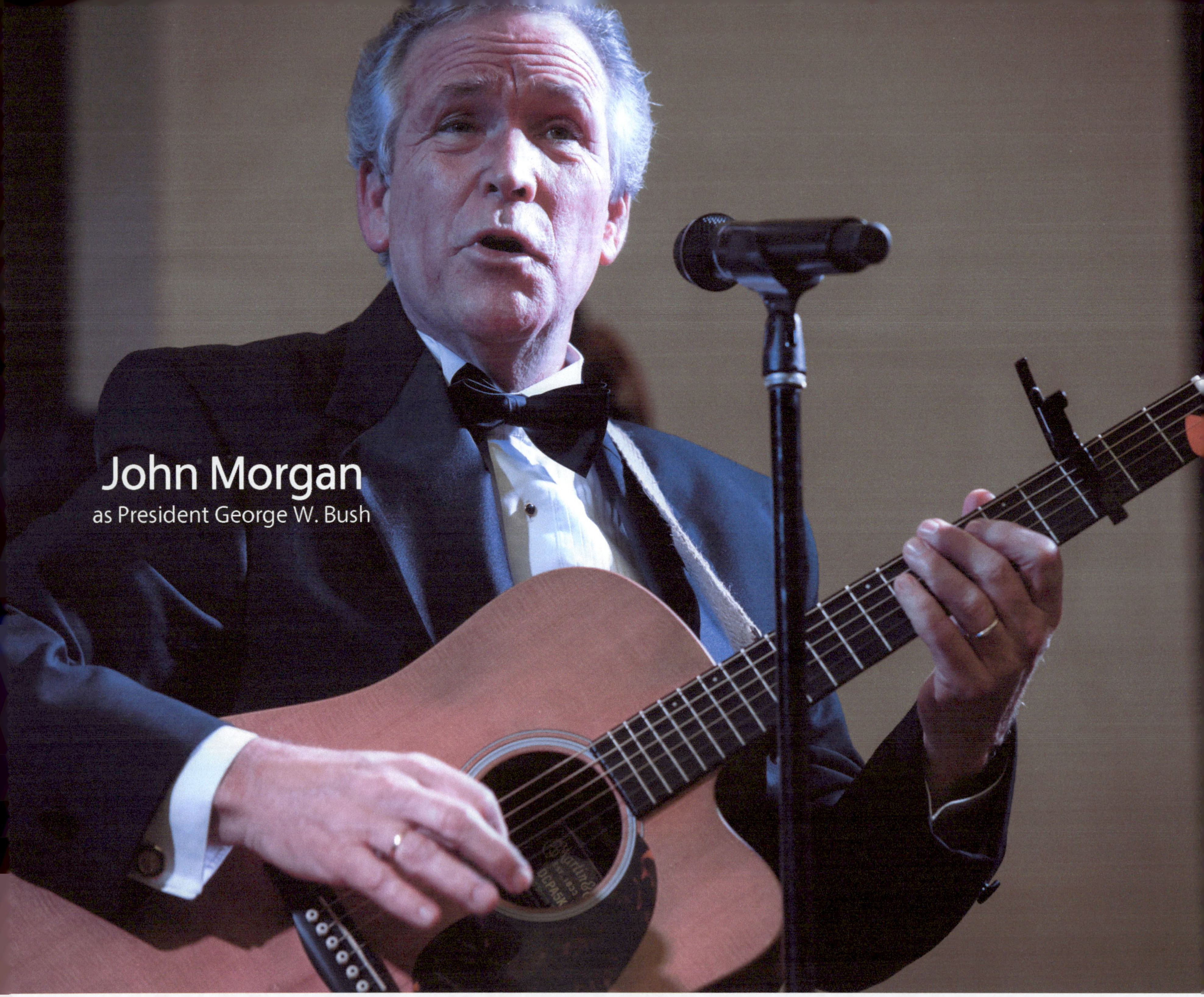

John Morgan
as President George W. Bush

TIME HAS BEEN KIND TO PRESIDENT GEORGE BUSH. He is remembered rather affectionately in the hearts and minds of many Americans. The hair, the shrug, the speech and expression are all present in John Morgan's extraordinary impersonation of Bush. And who knew the former President could play a guitar? Well, at least John can – and he often incorporates it into his presentation. A showman, musician, actor, author and comedian, John has appeared on *Good Morning America, The Today Show, America's Got Talent, Family Feud, Headline News, The Tony Danza Show, Hannity & Colmes, E! Entertainment Network, The View, The 700 Club* and more. Fans even voted him a finalist on ABC TV's celebrity reality show, *The Next Best Thing.* John was awarded America's # 1 Bush Impressionist along with two Mirror Image awards and a 2005 Cloney award for Best Historical Impersonation, voted on by his peers. He has also been featured on NPR's *All Things Considered*, and interviewed by dozens of newspapers such as *The Sunday London Times*. His comedic timing often accentuates a positive spiritual message shared with audiences worldwide. He has now added President Donald J. Trump to his repertoire. How does John feel about his unusual career path?

"It has been a tremendous privilege to impersonate President George W. Bush, and now, Donald J. Trump. When I began, I had no idea how much fun and how much satisfaction I would enjoy, not to mention that this career has provided a wonderful living for nearly 20 years," says John.

John has traveled worldwide and spoken to all size groups from small parties to large World Cup stadiums. "I've toured with large concert tours, Promise Keepers, Sean Hannity, Winter Jam, and spoken at all kinds of churches, corporations, associations, and non-profit events. I've gotten to meet presidents, movie stars and the world's most famous people. But better than all that, I've had the privilege of lifting up and encouraging millions of people around the globe. I've performed in China, Japan, Holland, and many other countries and nearly all fifty states. Long past George W. Bush's presidency, I've remained busy. And with Donald Trump, it continues!"

John keeps expanding his repertoire; he has developed a Willie Nelson impersonation and is working on other musical acts as well. But with his deadpan delivery, he could entertain people by impersonating Mr. Potato Head.

"Who knew that the lookalike industry would open so many, many doors and offer the privilege to influence to such a variety of people. It all began with a decision to move forward on something I thought I was created to do. You never know what doors will open for you in life. May God Bless you and may God bless America!"

"Being president is like running a cemetery: you've got a lot of people under you and nobody's listening." —William J. Clinton

Bettina Williams
as Whoopi Goldberg

Photos © Devon Cass
Author of *Double Take* by Devon Cass with John Filimon

"I WORK AS AN OFFICIAL COURT REPORTER for a District Judge. I have been a court reporter for almost 30 years. As a court reporter, my natural lookalike appearance can sometimes be distracting to jurors. Upon conclusion of some trials, the Judge normally thanks the jurors for their time and service, then asks them if they have any questions or comments. But sometimes, the Judge, expecting to explain some detail or nuance of the justice system, will recognize a juror who timidly raises their hand and asks, 'May I have a picture taken with your court reporter, Whoopi?' "

Bettina's impersonation career really began in 1993, after having had her hair braided with braid extensions, prior to vacationing in the Caribbean Islands with some friends. When they arrived, Bettina and her friends suddenly noticed that the islanders were unusually kind and friendly towards them. "We were literally blown away by the generosity and attention bestowed upon us. Particularly at this certain restaurant where we dined every night; the dinners were complimentary, as well as the champagne or drinks. We thought, "What a great island! These people are so wonderful and kind! We must tell everyone what a great vacation spot this is!"

Towards the end of the vacation, the mystery was solved. "The owner of the restaurant approached us and announced, 'The dinner is on the house again. And thank you so much for visiting our establishment, Ms. Goldberg. It has been an honor to serve you.' "

Bettina asked herself, "Who is Ms. Goldberg? I thought he had mistaken me for another woman that lived on the island. So in the confusion, we looked up and noticed, again, that people were still smiling and waving at us. That's when we realized what was really happening—I had been mistaken for the infamous Whoopi! Afraid that we would get busted, we hurriedly finished our meal and drinks, and ran—no, sprinted—out of the restaurant."

The following year in 1994, Bettina was encouraged by a close friend to enter a nationwide lookalike contest held by MGM in Las Vegas. Participants were narrowed down to 20 of the top lookalikes from all around the United States who were then flown to Las Vegas for the $10,000 reward.

"Prior to this, I never knew that a lookalike world even existed. Walking into that room and meeting other lookalikes, I was absolutely blown away. The Michael Jackson lookalike won the Grand Prize and I won 1st Runner-up. But within the audience were agents and my career, as a lookalike, took off from there."

There have certainly been some rewarding moments; "I was in California doing a gig with a Robin Williams lookalike. Afterwards, the clients took us to eat. As we were leaving the establishment and had almost made it to the cars, a woman ran behind us yelling 'Whoopi, Whoopi!' I started to turn around and tell her that I was sorry, but I was not Whoopi Goldberg. But when I faced her, she was already crying. She said, 'I can't believe I am finally seeing you again. I just wanted to tell you 'thank you.' I said, 'Thank me for what, baby?' She said, 'For saving my mother's life. When you came last year to Florida, you spoke about breast cancer. Well, that night my mother discovered a lump in her breast. Right away she went to get checked and the lump in her breast was cancer, but the doctor said she had caught it in time. So, Whoopi, if it wasn't for you, and my mother believing in you, she might have died.' "

Bettina says that they hugged for quite a long time and cried. "I have never felt so honored and humbled before in my life. We don't know what else our celebrities do. All we see are the movies and TV shows. But the devotion and dedication they have toward other projects is notable and honorable."

What are some of Bettina's other experiences as a lookalike? "One day, I was sitting out on the Riverwalk in San Antonio having lunch with a friend and saw someone running towards us. When the person finally approached, he yelled in my face, 'Mufasa!' I just looked at him as though he had lost his mind. He looked disappointed and then slowly walked away."

Later at work, she told someone about the incident. "It was parents bring-your-children-to-work-day and one of the little girls said, 'Bettina, that's from the movie, *The Lion King*. When they would say 'Mufasa' to Whoopi's character, she would respond as though she was afraid of the name and say, 'Ooooh, say it again!' Then I remembered exactly what she was talking about. And now I wish someone would say it to me again, because now I am ready. But to my own disappointment, it has never happened again!"

So has Bettina ever met Whoopi? "I have never met Whoopi Goldberg. But everyone who has, always tells me how cool and down-to-earth she is, and such a true authentic person. Even if I had not resembled Ms. Goldberg, I have always been a big fan and admirer of her work, from her one-woman show to *The View* and beyond. She represents so many women (and men) who just want to be their authentic self and be accepted for who they are. And it has been an honor, privilege, and an incredible journey impersonating her.

"Normal is just a cycle on the washing machine." —Whoopi Goldberg

Taylor Copenhaver
as Eminem

MARSHALL BRUCE MATHERS III, AMERICAN rapper, songwriter, and record producer is known professionally as Eminem. Among the best-selling music artists of all time with estimated worldwide sales of over 220 million records, he is credited with breaking racial barriers and popularizing hip hop in Middle America. He has been called one of the greatest rappers of all time.

"I first became aware of my resemblance to the legendary rapper in 2010 when the *Recovery* album was released. Friends would tell me 'You look just like him!' but I paid no attention for several years. Then I attended a convention for celebrity impersonators and my life changed dramatically. I went from a shy kid who was bullied and always got cut from sports because I was too skinny, to rapping in front of thousands of people. I now do Meet & Greet events as well as live tribute shows. Almost every time I go to the bank or grocery store someone makes a comment about 'Oh, Eminem's here again!' Or someone will ask the inevitable 'Do you know who you look like?'"

Taylor says one of his favorite things to do is to go out in public and get reactions from people. "They go crazy when they think they are meeting Eminem. It's an absolute blast and a trip. I have not met the real Eminem yet but that is one of my goals. I also want to make my own hip-hop music along with paying tribute to his music."

Taylor feels he is "blessed to be a part of this industry. It's been an amazing, life-changing ride."

"The truth is you don't know what is going to happen tomorrow. Life is a crazy ride, and nothing is guaranteed." —Eminem

Scott Mason
as Dame Edna

Photo © Peter Kuo and Michael Cairns

Scott F. Mason

SCOTT MASON HAD WORKED IN LOCAL AND REGIONAL theatre for twenty years before ever thinking about impersonating a celebrity. He minored in theatre in college where he began his trifecta of actor, director, and playwright; skills that would later bode him well in a second career as an impersonator.

Early in the Millennium, Scott was invited to a theatre friend's annual Halloween party that always had a theme. At this particular party, the theme was 'come as someone of the opposite gender that had a tv show.' It was then that Scott decided to try being Dame Edna whose imported BBC show had been a favorite of his when he would watch it following the *Benny Hill Show* as a teenager. The character, developed by multi-talented Australian actor, author and comedian Barry Humphries, is an outrageous, flamboyant, aging femme fatale - or at least thinks she is - with outsized glasses, gaudy gowns and pinkish-purple hair. Scott spray- painted a white wig pink, found a pair of glittery glasses and a sequin dress from a costume closet. During the party he did the voice (despite not a very convincing look) and the guests were thrilled. They suggested he do the impersonation for the local community theatre. In 2003 he made the first of many appearances at the Chapel Street Players as 'the Dame' delivering their welcome speech. Patrons soon asked him to do a full show which he did successfully in 2004 and 2005.

In 2008 a friend suggested that Scott attend an impersonators convention in Las Vegas. As part of a newcomer's showcase, Scott did about ten minutes of original comedy as Dame Edna and received a standing ovation. While there, he heard about a similar convention in Orlando, Florida. In Orlando later that year, Scott earned an award for Funniest Male Performer. Returning over the next six years, he won more awards for Funniest Male, Best Transformation, and Best Male Costume. In addition, Scott won two Outstanding Showcase awards as well and was inducted into a special Hall of Fame category for winning so many awards. He also made his way back to Vegas where he won another award for Best Comedian in 2010 and 2012.

BUT, perhaps the most significant honor for Scott came in 2010 when he auditioned for the title of the real Dame Edna's Honorary Understudy. The real Dame Edna, Mr. Humphries, was appearing with Michael Feinstein in spring of 2010 in a show called *All About Me*. As part of the marketing, the producers held an audition on Broadway in the theatre where the show was being produced to choose the Dame's understudy. The winner would appear in the Playbill and also do fun marketing events with the Dame. Scott attended the auditions in February along with about a dozen other contestants. They were judged by Michael Musto of the *Village Voice* as well as other NY critics and finally by both Feinstein and Humphries himself. Scott won the competition and got to spend the day talking with Humphries while he rehearsed. Alas, Scott never did get to do any marketing as the show closed after two weeks, however he did get to be in the Playbill and meet and be accepted by the man/character he impersonates, which is a rare treat in the impersonator world.

Since earning the title, Scott's 'second career' has really taken off with gigs throughout the country where he does a full two-hour show of original material as well as some of the real Dame's classic lines. He has had to sometimes break the hearts of some guests who believe him to be the real original Dame Edna, despite the fact that marketing material for shows list Scott as impersonating the Dame. Finally,

Scott's Dame Edna appeared in both the award winning short and long subject documentary *Just About Famous* so he is thrilled to now be listed on the IMDB, a popular, online database of information related to films, television programs and more where he will hopefully be eternally viewed.

"I'm approaching 70. Unfortunately, from the wrong direction." —Barry Humphries

Photo © Troy Nelson

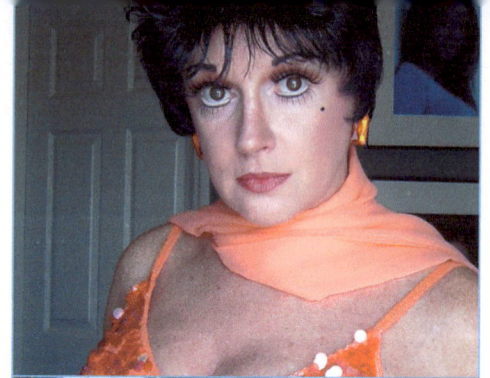

5th Gear

Jennifer Ramsey
as Lucy, Liza, Judge Judy, and Bette Davis

Photos © Geri Muck, Dollar Store, and Brian Howell

WITH A BACKGROUND IN THEATER AND MURDER MYSTERY entertainment as well as hairstyling and make-up, in 1994 Jennifer won the World Tribute Artists Championship Award for her impersonation of Marilyn Monroe, an award that really changed her life in regards to being an entertainer.

She has now been in the Celebrity Tribute industry for over 20 years. Jennifer impersonates so many different characters that she was inducted into the Hall of Fame in 2014 for winning the Sybil Award three times at the Sunburst Convention for Professional Celebrity Impersonators. She also won the Transformation award in 2013.

Some of the characters she portrays are Nancy Pelosi, Liza Minnelli, Lucy, Joan Rivers, Bette Davis, Joan Crawford, Elvira, Judge Judy, and many others. She is also the owner and founder of Ramsey's Replicas, a production company that presents the best in Celebrity Tribute entertainment, murder mysteries, and a variety of shows. In 2014, she was nominated for Agent of the Year. Jennifer has done film, print, commercials, television and voiceover work as well and says "It has been my honor to portray the stars that people love and what a pleasure to meet and work with so many wonderful and creative people."

Indeed, versatile Jennifer can be so many wonderful and creative people herself, that others say it's a pleasure to work with her, whichever personality she assumes.

"An actor is an impersonator; he plays many different roles. If you played the same role all the time, God - that'd be a boring career. When you take on different roles and become a different person, that's called acting... It's a challenge."

—Robert Loggia

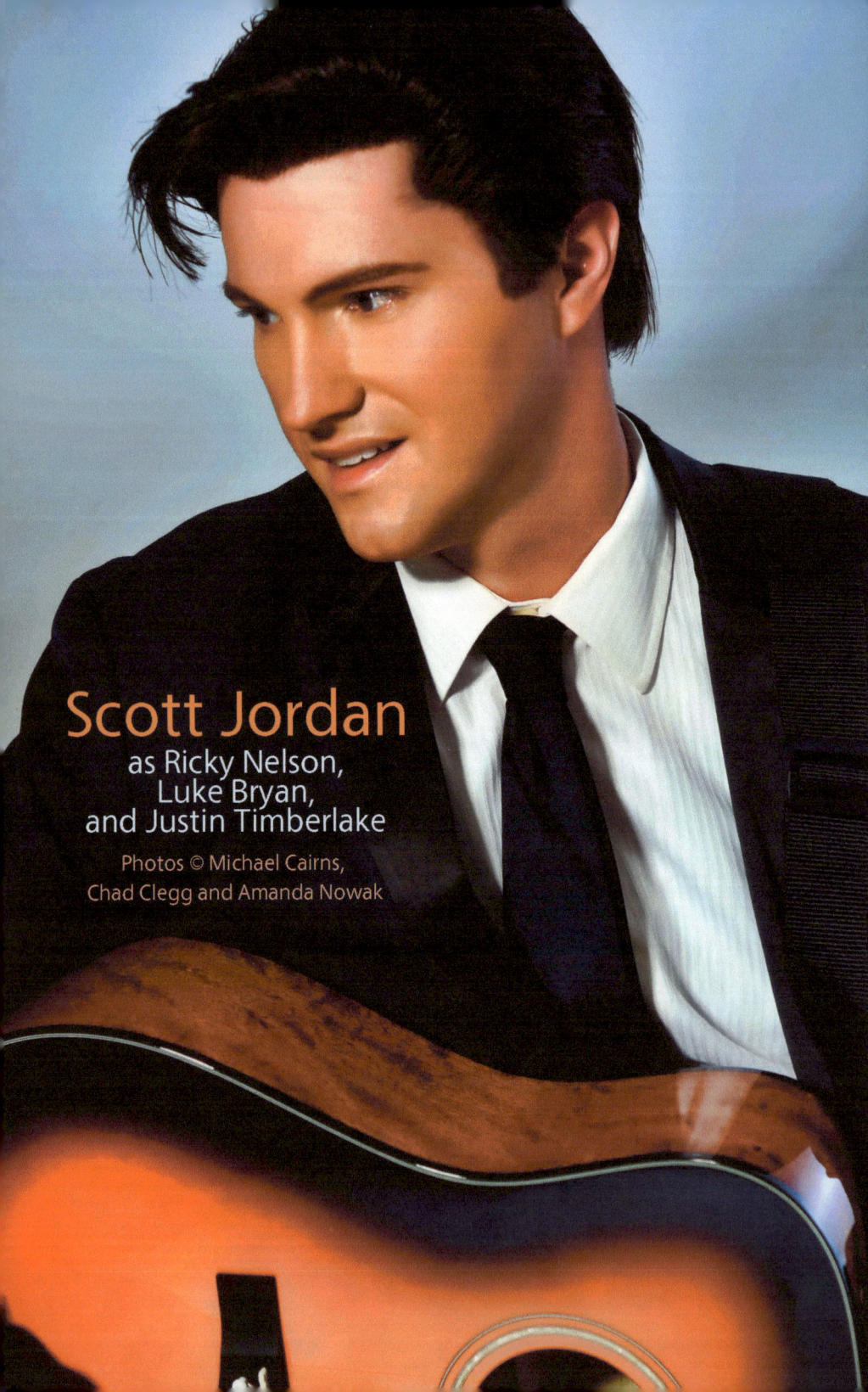

PLAY IT AGAIN

A TRIBUTE TO CHART-TOPPING COUNTRY MUSIC STAR

LUKE BRYAN

Scott Jordan
as Ricky Nelson, Luke Bryan, and Justin Timberlake

Photos © Michael Cairns, Chad Clegg and Amanda Nowak

MULTI-TALENTED SCOTT JORDAN is a man of many faces. He wears them all well.

Q. How did you get started in this business?

"Well, I started performing NSYNC songs when I was in college, then I was singing some Justin Timberlake songs in the *Chippendales* show in Europe and Vegas and *Legends in Concert* was looking for a Timberlake. They heard about me, I auditioned, and ten years later here we are. Not a day goes by, that I am not humbled and proud to have been able to start my career in that show. A few years ago I decided to step outside the box a bit and create my own Justin Timberlake tribute show called *Mirrors.* It's a 90-minute labor of love and my band and I have been fortunate to perform that show from coast to coast."

Q. Is Justin Timberlake the only character you do??

"Timberlake is my primary character but I also do Ricky Nelson and country star Luke Bryan."

Q. Ricky Nelson?

"Growing up I had a wide variety of musical influences and one of them was Ricky Nelson. My Mom and Dad and grandparents introduced me to that era of music and I just fell in love with Ricky and the entire Nelson family. I wanted to add an older artist to my repertoire to increase bookings and add a different demographic to my audience, as well as make myself more valuable to *Legends in Concert.* There were already many people doing Elvis so I thought Ricky Nelson made perfect sense and I put an audition video together. About a year later, I debuted Ricky Nelson at *Legends in Concert.* Justin Timberlake fans and Luke Bryan fans are usually around the same age so I can often double book myself in the same weekend, at the same venue."

Q. Out of the three, which one is the most challenging?

"Luke is definitely the hardest of my three acts to perform just because his voice is so different than mine but I have an absolute blast performing his songs."

Q. How do you get into character playing these different guys?

"Timberlake is easy. I've been doing it for so long it's just like flipping a switch and I'm on. With Luke Bryan, his voice is so unique and so different from mine that I have to practice for about an hour before I start, all the way up to the time I go on. Ricky is a complete transformation. I have to shave and I wear a lot of makeup and I have this amazing wig that completes the look. I generally watch a little Ozzie and Harriet while I'm doing my makeup to get into his character."

Q. What is your favorite part of the job?

"Being able to make people happy through music. I have such a blast doing each character for different reasons. I love seeing the smiles in the crowd when I am doing Ricky and just taking these people back to some great memories. And seeing my oldest daughter's face as she watches her Daddy on stage is just the most amazing thing."

"There's nothing wrong with shooting for the stars." —Justin Timberlake

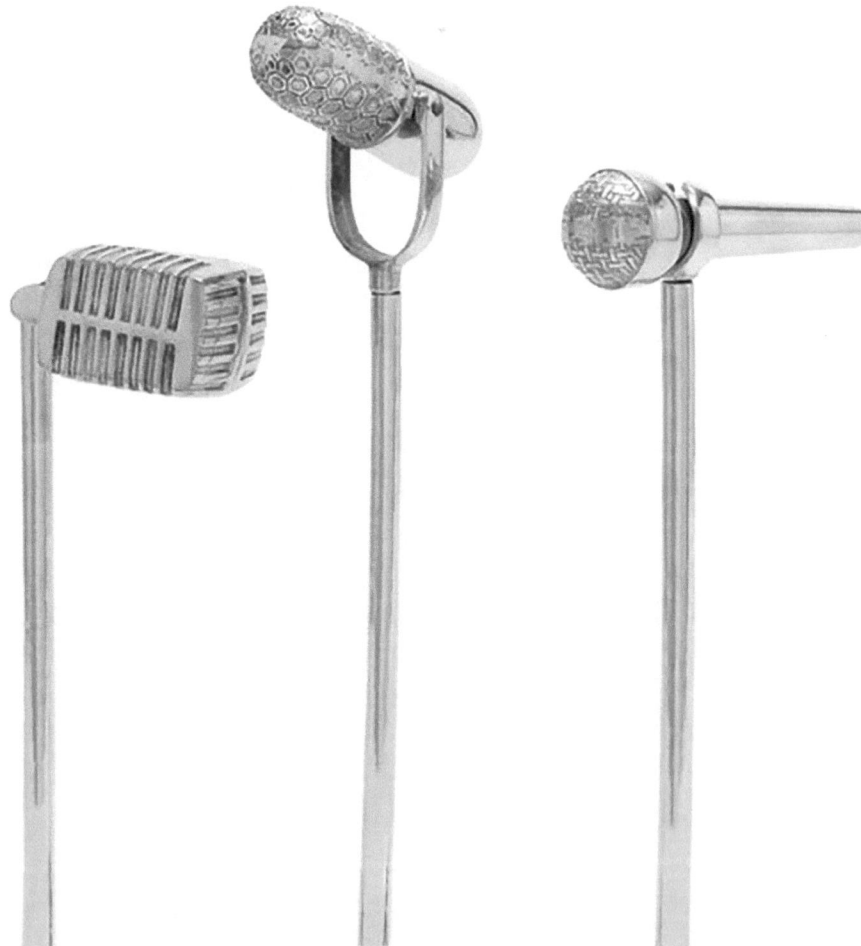

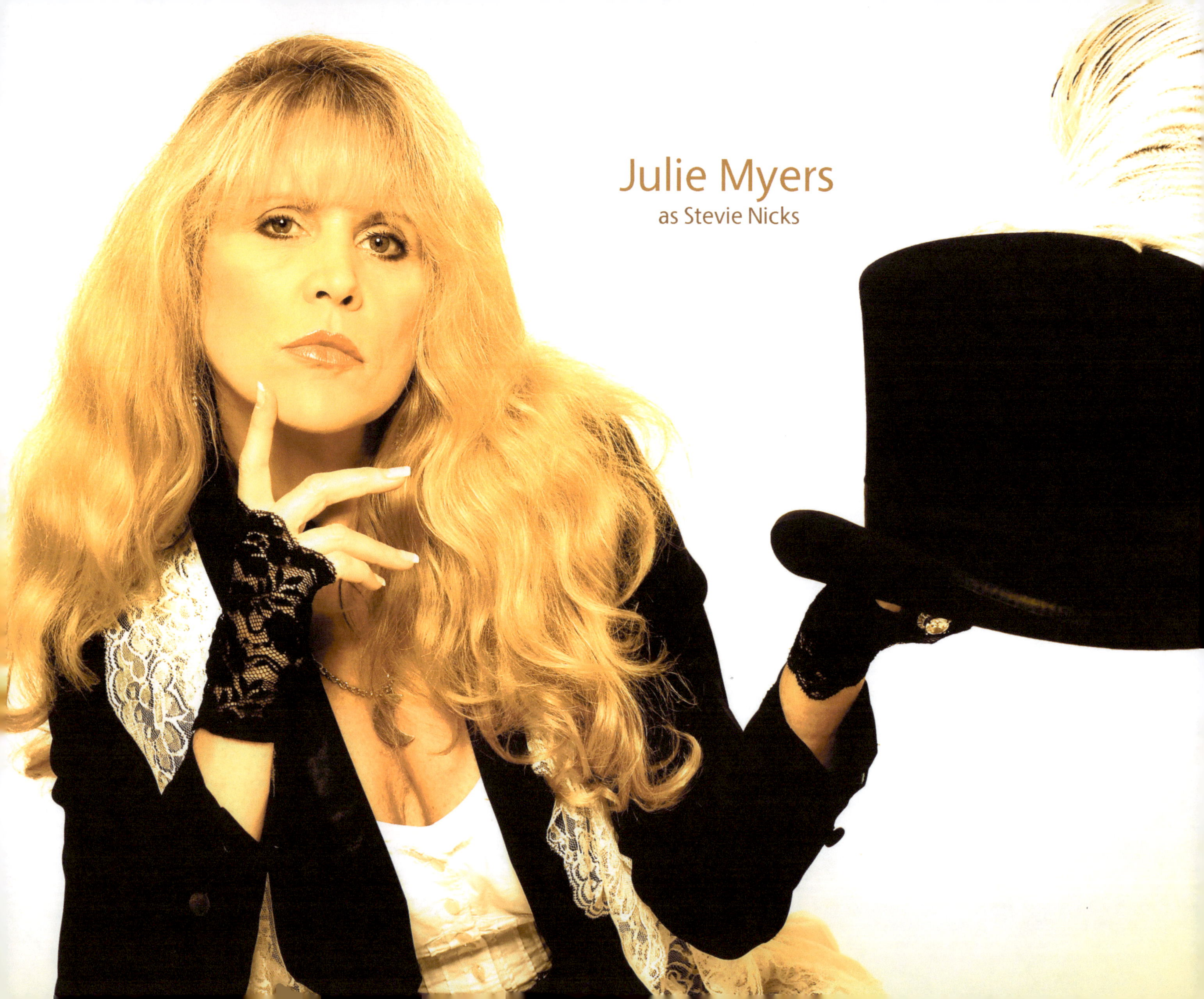

Julie Myers
as Stevie Nicks

"YEARS AGO I WAS WORKING OUT of Vegas with the tribute show *Legends in Concert* as a backup singer/dancer. I remember not really understanding why anyone would want to perform as someone else other than themselves. It didn't make a lot of sense to me until I worked and traveled with many of these people for a few years. If you were lucky enough to resemble someone famous and talented enough to sound and move like them, you could make pretty good money and travel the world doing it. It's an acting job. "

Julie continues, "I had been retired from a professional dance career for nearly a decade but often dreamed of getting back into the entertainment business. However, I had no clue what the first step in that direction would look like. About ten years ago, after I had my hair heavily highlighted and cut my bangs, people started telling me that I resembled Stevie Nicks. I was approached daily everywhere I went; restaurants, airports, public restrooms. Was fate trying to lend me a hand here?" Julie wondered if her dreams of becoming a performer again and seeing the world were being answered.

"Ten years later, as Stevie Nicks, I have had some pretty amazing experiences. I have been chased down Time Square in New York by fans, posed for countless pictures that I know probably became someone's lie about meeting the real Stevie, I was a surprise for a bride at a lesbian wedding, performed karaoke in drag bars and sang with the Dallas Symphony. I have performed for upper echelon corporate executive functions as well as in the smokiest and smallest of bars. I have sung in front of thousands of people and audiences where I could count the attendance on one hand."

She continues, "I have been treated like royalty, served fine wine and taxied by limo. I have been put up in the most expensive hotel suites and I have stayed in roach-infested motels with not even water to drink back stage and was lucky if I could get taxi fare to the airport."

Julie says "I've met a lot of interesting people since starting in this crazy business. Some awesome, professional, inspiring, talented, genuine people with a love of entertainment in common. I have also met some not so genuine, backstabbing, lying, stealing, fake people as well. Like anything else you gotta weigh the good with the bad and take a lot of what is said and heard with a grain of salt. It's not everyone's cup of tea and you have to develop a thick skin!"

"The question I get asked the most is 'Have you ever met Stevie Nicks?' I suppose it would be a dream come true for most tribute artists, to meet whomever you pay tribute to and if you should get an approval or endorsement from the star; even better. Unfortunately, not every music icon is flattered by a spot-on impersonator and some are actually put off by them. As I said, it's not everyone's cup of tea," says Julie.

"I have never met Stevie but I have met her best friend, her ex-husband and fellow Fleetwood Mac band member Mick Fleetwood. All were blown away at my resemblance and all had the power to introduce me to her. Let's just say the time was never right."

Julie says she has the utmost respect for Stevie and her music and that she has really changed her life. "Imitation IS the highest form of flattery and I am introducing a lot of people to her music for the first time and giving them a live show that they can afford, sometimes in a small town or venue that Stevie would never perform in. Paying tribute to the Queen of Rock and Roll has influenced me and helped me to become a better performer all the way around and I will continue to do it as long as people want me to. It is fun to play dress up and portray a rock icon on stage! I love entertaining people and making them smile! I LOVE ROCK AND ROLL!

"The music business is a cruel and shallow money trench, a long plastic hallway where thieves and pimps run free, and good men die like dogs. There's also a negative side." —Hunter S. Thompson

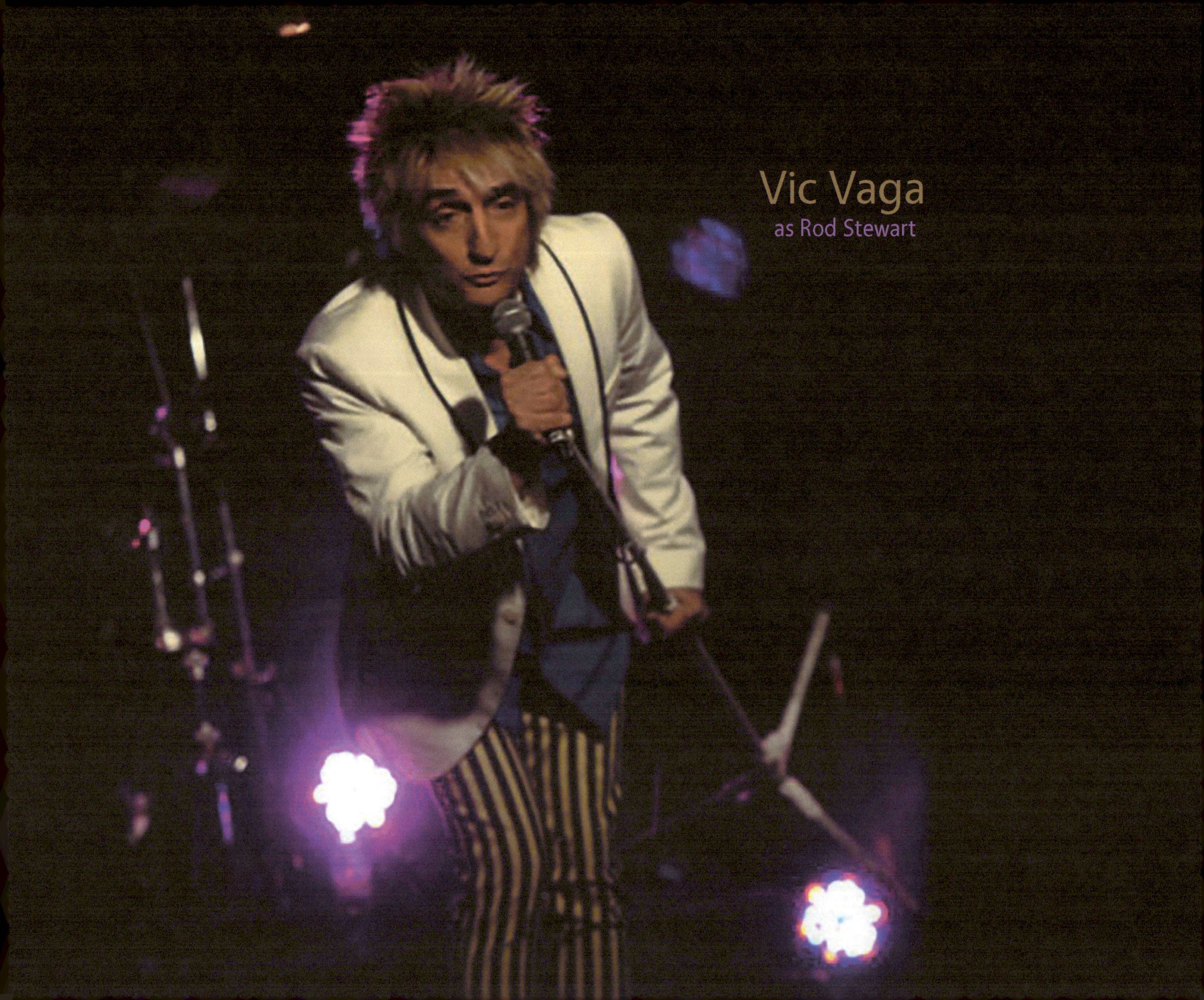

Vic Vaga

as Rod Stewart

Q. How did you get started being a Rod Stewart tribute artist?

"In response to being constantly teased by sorority girls about my resemblance to rock star Rod Stewart, I dared to dress as Rod for a fraternity Halloween party. That night was memorable to say the least, so on subsequent Halloweens, I donned the costume again and again. I was winning first place everywhere I went. I even won a car one year. It was at one of these parties that a celebrity lookalike agent 'discovered' me and eventually convinced me to become a Rod lookalike/impersonator. Since then I have played all sorts of venues, including being the warm-up for a pig race."

Q. Have you ever been nervous about the crowd reaction to you as Rod?

"I am mistaken for Rod often. I went to see his concert in Montreal. As I walked in, the crowd got a bit over excited and frenzied as I walked to my seat. The whole arena thought I was him. It was the first time that I had ever been frightened by the huge response.

Q. As Rod, have you had any funny incidents or particularly memorable appearances?

"At a venue one night, a lady decided to put some tip money in the front of my spandex trousers. She then proceeded to pull my trousers down as I was performing, therefore giving the crowd way more than they expected that night."

Q. Do you do any other characters or celebrities?

"Rod is the only character I do, although since the early '80s I've been told that I resemble Steve Perry of Journey, Ronnie Wood of the Rolling Stones/Faces, Barry Manilow, CC DeVille of Poison…"

"If you want my body and you think I'm sexy
Come on, honey, tell me so
If you really need me just reach out and touch me
Come on, sugar, let me know"

—Rod Stewart, *Do You Think I'm Sexy?*

105

Greg Thompson
as Andy Warhol,
Austin Powers,
and Santa

GREG THOMPSON has worn many hats in the entertainment industry. He has a diverse background as an entertainer and motivational speaker. He has been a musician, emcee, talent agent, stage manager and more. As Executive Producer of the Annual Sunburst Convention of Celebrity Impersonators, he has helped to shape and guide the careers of many of the individuals on these pages.

An expert in the field of celebrity impersonation, Thompson says he can clearly see the industry growing, just within the last 15 years. "The look-alike phenomenon started as a unique entertainment option and has now developed into a billion-dollar industry," he says.

Greg knows first-hand how to step into a role that has already been created because he plays such characters as diverse as Andy Warhol, Austin Powers, Jack Sparrow and SANTA CLAUS! That's right, Greg also runs a seasonal Santa booking agency. Who knew Santa had an agent? And what celebrity could be more recognizable than Santa?! Greg performs as Santa Claus himself and trains other entertainers so they can work as the jolly, loveable, red-suited St. Nick. Greg can arrange personalized Santa visits during the holidays and even offers a 'bad Santa' for more sophisticated crowds.

But Thompson says he has the most fun playing Austin Powers because he can get away with saying and doing so much that he couldn't as himself. As far as the celebrity impersonators he works with, Greg feels that those who conscientiously work on and develop their characters properly are the most successful. He has been in the position of seeing these performers polish their acts, try out new characters and mature into seasoned professionals. The Sunburst Convention offers chances to learn about all aspects of the business but even more importantly, it provides a community of support. Some of the attendees act as informal mentors to the inexperienced, thus raising the bar for the industry in general. Knowledge is shared, networking occurs, friendships and partnerships flourish.

Says Greg, ""This industry is full of some of the most genuine and kind people you've ever met... even when pretending to be other people."

The convention also includes showcases for agents, event planners and buyers who are looking for talent but which are open to the public.

"You know, Dr. Evil, I have always thought you were crazy, but now I can see you're nuts." —Austin Powers

Joe Passion
as Jerry Lee Lewis

ORIGINALLY FROM TORONTO, Canada, Joe Passion tours internationally in the USA, Europe, England and Australia. He performs mainly as Jerry Lee Lewis but does other tributes as well, including Barry Manilow, John Lennon, Dion Demucci and Jimmy Buffett to name a few. Passion has been performing as a tribute artist for the past 20 years and was a professional musician, singer, songwriter, and arranger for over 15 years before that. He has been an opening act for The Who, Procol Harum, The Band, Johnny Winter, Bonnie Tyler, Devine, Hot Chocolate, Sha-Na-Na and Poco with Jim Messina.

"When I first started playing music, at nine years of age, "Whole Lotta Shaking" and "Great Balls of Fire," both by Jerry Lee Lewis, were the first rock 'n roll songs I ever learned on piano. "Twist and Shout" and "Hard Days Night" were my first songs on guitar."

Joe says that many years later he found himself as the bandleader and musical director of a Toronto dinner theater, his first steady gig in a career of one-nighters. The show was called *Rock & Roll Heaven*.

"I was playing boogie piano for the Elvis impersonator and was hamming it up. The band was off on the side of the stage so the audience could easily see what we were doing. I was very visible. Years of fronting my own bands were hard to forget and even though I had that steady paycheck as musical director, I couldn't resist the temptation of working with the headliners. It was fun. Then people began coming up to me at the end of the night and telling me how much they enjoyed my performance, saying I played just like Jerry Lee Lewis, so why didn't I do Jerry in the show? My gypsy blood was beginning to boil."

People kept paying him the same kinds of compliments repeatedly, almost to the point of embarrassment, he says. "So… I went to the producer of the show when the cast was changing and I knew there would be an opening to make my suggestion. 'Why don't you let me try Jerry Lee in the Show?' he asked."

At the time the cast had an Elvis, Buddy Holly, Richie Valens, Roy Orbison and Big Bopper. "I thought a Jerry Lee would be perfect. But the producer looked at me and said 'Joe …Jerry Lee is still alive! This show is called *Rock & Roll HEAVEN!!*' I was embarrassed to say the least, but the flame was lit, so to speak, and I continued with my idea. Honestly at the time I'm sure I was partially motivated by the extra money and new opportunities of fame and fortune."

Then Joe designed and built, with some help, a prop piano that his electric grand would fit inside. He then designed the front leg to collapse, as the finale to his act would appear to involve destroying the piano - something Jerry Lee Lewis was known for as well as kicking the stool. Then he took his invention to a local pyro-tech company and had the piano fitted for fire. "ITS GOTTA BURN!" he said.

But shortly after, he heard the show was looking for a John Lennon and they were going to bring someone in from Vegas. "*BIG BUCKS!!* I thought. Here's my second chance. I had played in a Beatle Band in my earlier club days so the Lennon character was already rehearsed… well… comfortable anyway. My wife thought I was crazy. I went out and bought wigs, clothes, a Rickenbacker guitar and did a demo of Lennon and Beatles songs in my studio, playing everything myself. I walked into the office at the theater and in my best Liverpool accent, I said 'Yeh – um,…I'm - ah, here to apply for the John Lennon role in your show, man….yeh, it's what I do, yeh….so how about it?' For a few minutes, they didn't know it was Joe.

"Then we all had a good laugh and they gave me a shot, an audition they called it. At the time I thought audition ME!? Don't you know who I think I am?!! However, everything worked out and I got the gig. I also managed to sneak Jerry Lee in the show. They did it by announcing, 'This is as close to HEAVEN as 'the Killer' is ever going to get…. Ladies and gentlemen, Jerry Lee Lewis.' Thus began my new performing career as a Legends entertainer."

Joe continues, "All my life people would say 'You know who you look like?' They may see another character in me that I never thought of. My main character these days is Jerry Lee, then Barry Manilow and of course, John Lennon," he says. "I look at the tribute world as a musical acting gig. I am a member of ACTRA and unlike some of my peers that are still playing local gigs, I've always focused on music when in the studio and performance when on the stage. So re-creating these characters and adding my own slant is not much different than doing *Hamlet* or *Twelfth Night*…well not <u>too</u> much anyway…"

He stayed at Rock & Roll Heaven on and off for four years.

"I went to see Jerry Lee in concert a few years back. I met the band; Kenny Lovelace, James Burton (of Elvis fame) and Slim Jim Phantom of the Stray Cats. They were hot! Jerry had already left the building by the time I got in the dressing room but I still keep in touch with Kenny. I hope to see and meet Jerry in person someday. I think he's great and I'm also a fan."

"If I'm going to Hell, I'm going there playing the piano." —Jerry Lee Lewis

Bill Pantazis
as George Michael

UK-BASED GEORGE MICHAEL first achieved musical success in 1981 as half of the duo WHAM! He later went on to become a star in his own right and one of the world's best-selling music artists, selling more than 100 million records worldwide as of 2010. A singer, songwriter, multi-instrumentalist and producer, he has won multiple awards and in 2005, was the subject of a documentary; A Different Story, which covered his personal life and professional career.

Canadian Bill Pantazis is not only a fan, but a dead-ringer for Michael.

During George Michael's last North American tour in 2008, Bill was fortunate enough to see him in both Las Vegas and Vancouver. "The Las Vegas concert was first. As we were leaving someone stopped me just outside the exit doorway and asked to have a photo taken together. One photo led to another . . . and another . . . and another . . . until over an hour went by of constant photo taking."

At the Vancouver concert, they had floor seats, fourth row center stage. "Before the concert began, again someone asked me for a photo. Before I knew it, there was a line of people down the aisle waiting to have their photo taken with me. Security decided this was not a good idea and told everyone to go back to their seats. The security guard then politely told me that I was too much of a distraction and I needed to stay seated and face forward. But that was only after he and his partner had their photo taken with me!"

The most meaningful and rewarding experience he has had as George was being at the bedside of a 30-year-old man who was dying of cancer. "There was a George Michael concert a week away and his family had asked me to stop by and see him because he was a huge George Michael fan. When I walked into the room he was wearing a 25 LIVE George Michael T-shirt. When he saw me, his eyes widened as he uttered 'George Michael!' I believe that may have been one of his more memorable moments, prior to passing just a few days later. I know it was one of mine."

Ya gotta have faith.

"And it's hard to love, there's so much to hate
Hanging on to hope
When there is no hope to speak of
And the wounded skies above say it's much too late
Well maybe we should all be praying for time"

—George Michael, Praying for Time

Ted Torres Martin
as Elvis Presley

PERHAPS NO ONE IS MORE REVERED, copied and beloved than the King of Rock 'n Roll; Elvis Presley. Immediately recognizable worldwide, in all his incarnations and each era of his fabled career, he took the world by storm with his style, powerful vocals and sheer charisma. Of course, it helped that he was drop-dead gorgeous.

It is no mystery why the desire to portray Elvis is a goal for many. The challenge lies in the ability. A true Presley Tribute Artist must come close to capturing the elusive but awesome stage presence, confidence and animal magnetism the King exuded. It is a mix of humble origins, spirituality and that undefined characteristic often called 'star quality,' a tall order for anyone.

Among other honors, Elvis Tribute Artist Ted Torres Martin won Images Of The King World Champion in 2016, Heart Of The King Award at The Las Vegas Hilton in 2014 and The Spirit Of The King Award presented by Elvis Presley Enterprises. He has done other characters such as Ricky Nelson but focuses on Presley.

Q. How did you get started in this business and why Elvis?

"I always say I'm an Elvis fan first, because I am! I am a true 100% Elvis Presley Fan. I'm a singer/musician/songwriter/actor. People kept telling me I sounded like Elvis when I sang. I entered a small Elvis contest and won. Gordon Stoker from The Jordanaires, Elvis' back-up singers, told me I could probably do something with it. So I took his advice."

Q. What was the first Elvis song you ever heard and how old were you?

"I was about 10 years old when I heard my dad playing some old cassettes in our garage. The song was "Silver Bells." I asked my dad who that was singing and he said Elvis Presley. I didn't revisit Elvis' music again until 2 years later but I always remembered that moment."

Q. Any particularly memorable gigs?

"I have played all over the world. In Daytona Beach I played to a crowd of about 6,500 to 7,000 people one time. But as for a single moment, it has to be playing the stage where Elvis performed at the old Las Vegas Hilton, now Westgate Las Vegas, and getting an award presented to me on that very stage. It was a very special moment."

Q. Elvis' career spanned many years; Do you have a preference as to which 'Elvis era' you enjoy performing most?

"I really enjoy portraying Elvis from 1968 'til around 1971, even though I can sing every era. Those years showcase my best Elvis look."

Q. What are some funny stories you can remember about performing as Elvis?

"I know how Elvis felt at times! It's always funny when ladies throw panties or bras on stage! They make me turn red for sure."

Q. Any particularly memorable people you have met on this journey?

"I have been so lucky in this industry. I have met and shared the stage with so many people that have shared the stage with Elvis and knew him very well. The Jordanaires, DJ Fontana, The Sweet Inspirations, The Stamps quartet - I have shared the stage with all of them at some point in my career. People I have met who have been very kind have been Chris Isaak, Frankie Valli, Engelbert Humperdinck, Wayne Newton… the list goes on. I really have been very fortunate - moments I will always cherish for sure."

Q. How has playing the late great Elvis Presley impacted your life - or has it?

"Portraying Elvis has impacted my life in a really big way. I have met many great people that were part of Elvis' life, great Elvis fans, I have traveled the world, met my beautiful wife through Elvis' music and I have the life I have today because of him and his music. I'm very grateful to God, my parents, the real Elvis fans & the great Elvis Presley!"

"It would be interesting if Elvis were reincarnated as an Elvis impersonator." —Demetri Martin

Johnny Moroko

as Mick Jagger

Photo © Don Campbell Photography

"I FIRST NOTICED THE RESEMBLANCE AT AGE 13. There was a full-page picture of Mick in Newsweek magazine during the '72 tour. The very next day someone mentioned it, then I didn't hear it again until ladies mentioned it in bars. That was some pickup line..."

Johnny says, "Every time I grew my hair out, people always noticed it. I also, at various times, have resembled David Bowie and Kurt Cobain. That was during my blonde years. There's also a small faction of people who think I'm an absolute dead-ringer for Axl Rose. I kid you not. They're serious. This went on until one day, a dueling pianist in Reno stepped on an elevator and interrupted my friends and I twice to mention how much I looked like Mick. He said he was a former Jerry Lee Lewis tribute performer for Legends (I checked, he was), and he talked to me for five minutes. I dyed my hair two months later."

Johnny definitely has Mick's carnal strut and swagger as well as the cockney-infused vocals.

"It's taken a few years longer than I thought, but I'm comfortable with my skill and confidence level now. I chuckle when I think of how I wouldn't sit in with a band when I first started, and now you can't keep me off a stage!"

Johnny says he has been places where he really needed security. "Some people can't handle their alcohol and impersonators at the same time. Bob Saget even interrupted an event to walk over and tell me over the PA, how scary it was that I look like Mick Jagger. The more metropolitan the city, the more stops and photo ops happen. I've had football coach/commentators stare at me at gas stations. I've posed for a lot of pictures. I've had people sneer at me for being a wannabe."

He says he hasn't met Mick. "I'm not in it to meet him. It would be a lucky stroke for that to happen. I stay focused on the look, the music, the attitude and the voice. Singing requires a discipline that I work hard not to stray from. It's very hard work being Mick Jagger."

Johnny looks so much like Jagger that it's difficult to imagine him impersonating anyone else. "I've thought of doing multiple characters and have performed as Joey Ramone. Jim Morrison is possible..."

What does Johnny like best about being a celebrity Tribute Artist? "My lucky talent has allowed me to share a stage with truly talented artists and musicians. I get a close-up look at guitarists, drummers, bassists and keyboard players, and the joy I experience from sharing those moments with them and the audiences are what I look forward to at every performance, big or small. I make new friends everywhere I go, and life is pretty good."

"A good thing never ends." —Mick Jagger

Chris America
as Madonna

CHRIS AMERICA WAS THE ORIGINAL MADONNA IMPERSONATOR in the tribute industry dating back to March of 1984. At a time when MTV was brand new and the show *Putting on The Hits* was all the rage; Chris was the Madonna that agents sought after for live appearances to satisfy the star's ever-growing legion of ravenous fans. Prior to this, Chris worked as singing telegram talent in the early 80s while attending college. One afternoon, she was called into an office and told by her agent that impersonators were becoming a new trend in the event planning industry. The agent and her staff felt that Chris resembled a new rising star on the scene - Madonna - and suggested she give impersonating a try . . . and here is where Chris' lifelong career as a faux Madonna began.

"I had not even heard of her at the time but suddenly I was constantly being stopped on the street and people were reacting to me wherever I'd go." With only a new music video to reference, Chris pulled together the classic Madonna look and things took off from there, eventually to the point where Chris specialized as Madonna full time and it hasn't stopped since.

In her 30+ years of portraying the 'Material Girl,' Chris has had many unique opportunities. Most noted will always be her appearance as Madonna with child on the cover of *Esquire Magazine*, fooling many readers and at the time pulling in the highest editorial ratings in the magazine's history—Madonna herself even stating that Chris was a "...great representation." She went on to appear a few times on the *Oprah Winfrey Show*, was photographed by renowned fashion photographer Francesco Scavullo, stylized by John Freida and became a regular guest on all of the popular daytime talk shows. These appearances eventually led to entertainment contracts around the world, doubling as Madonna for VIPs at several concerts, a regular hire in Madison Square Garden's PR department to eventually performing for John Paul Gaultier's Touring Expo and headlining several years at New York City's Madonnathon. This included a special tribute show dedicated to Madonna on her 50th Birthday. She performed at Madonna's home town of Bay City Michigan in her honor and entertained at the White House in Washington DC and in Times Square on New Year's Eve in 2013.

Chris is a multi-award-winning tribute artist who was given the highest award in 2013 and top honors in her industry at the National Celebrity Impersonator's Convention for outstanding performance and portrayal of her character. In 2014 she was inducted into the Sunburst Celebrity Impersonator's Hall of Fame.

In 2015, she was featured in two documentaries, *Just About Famous* as a featured act in a film highlighting the profession of celebrity impersonators and *Mad for Madonna*, a film about those who hold unique standing in her international fan community. She met the star, sometimes known as the 'queen of pop' informally in 1995 and in 2013 her Manager Guy Oseary marveled at Chris' uncanny likeness, stating her physical look was "...incredible and eerily similar to Madonna's, especially in person."

121

Chris continues her journey as a full-time tribute artist; currently she is developing a road show that will highlight performances of Madonna's 30-year career complete with iconic costume styles spanning the early 80s all the way into the *Rebel Heart* tour and album release.

Chris is married and resides in the DC tri-state Area.

"I stand for freedom of expression, doing what you believe in, and going after your dreams." —Madonna

Michael Walter

as Don Rickles

A CERTAIN GENERATION OF PEOPLE WERE FAMILIAR with a certain kind of comedy – and a specific style of comedian. The stand-up of the 1960's was usually a master of the monologue, with a string of jokes at his fingertips.

Don Rickles was one of the few who broke the mold. After being honorably discharged from the Navy in 1946, Rickles studied at the American Academy of Dramatic Arts for two years, then played bit parts on television. Frustrated by a lack of acting work, Rickles began doing stand-up comedy, performing in clubs in New York, Miami, and Los Angeles. He became known as an 'insult comedian' by responding to his hecklers. Audiences enjoyed these acerbic insults more than his prepared material, and he incorporated them into his act. He not only heckled the hecklers but anyone who was in his line of fire, calling them hockey pucks, dummies and more. When the bald, tuxedoed, Rickles was onstage, anyone was a target. He poked fun of all ethnicities and walks of life and had a huge following throughout his career. In an interview with Jay Leno, Rickles was asked whether he ever feared his comedic style might become too offensive.

He replied, "You know, every night when I go out on stage, there's always one nagging fear in the back of my mind. I'm always afraid that somewhere out there, there is one person in the audience that I'm not going to offend!"

Mike "Wally" Walter has been doing comedy for 35 years. So how did he come to impersonate the man sarcastically known as Mr. Warmth? In his own words;

"In 2005 I was hired as a comedian at Harrah's Casino in Laughlin, Nevada. My performances consisted of eight, 12-minute sets a week. I got paid good money, was given a place to live and got meals at the casino. It was a dream gig. The one thing I kept hearing was that I reminded the audience of a cross between Don Rickles and Jonathan Winters, another comedic genius of the era. I considered this to be a huge compliment as I have always been a fan of both. Did I mention that in 2005, I had hair?"

He goes on, "Several years later, I watched a video of myself and noticed something odd. I was bald and looked similar to Rickles. People kept telling me I should become an impersonator of Don! Studying the great one, as I had come to think of him, I realized that my style was similar to his – a smart ass."

Purchasing a tuxedo, he tried some of Rickles patter in comedy rooms and it went over well. "Younger people know Rickles only from the *Toy Story* movies but the demographic of the people who really knew Don, loved what I did and remarked about how well I did him. Even comedian Bob Newhart, a friend of Rickles, upon meeting me said 'Do you know how much you look like Don Rickles?' "

After doing Don sporadically, in 2010, he found out Don was performing at a nearby casino in Washington, so he bought tickets to see him. "We were in the 23rd row. I had on my tuxedo and my lady was dressed to the nines. We arrived and heads turned as we walked toward the restaurant for dinner. Seated at our table people would walk by, do a double take then sheepishly approach to ask if they could get a picture with me. I obliged, telling them that I was an impersonator and not really Don. When we went into the showroom and took our seats, a gentleman from across the room sidled over to us with his walker."

"Sir," he said. "I watched you in 1977 in Vegas and I'm looking forward to seeing you again tonight!"

"You think *I'm* Rickles?" said Michael.

"You're not?" he asked.

"If I was, I could have gotten better seats!" Michael replied.

"The following year I asked an agent friend to call Don's road manager to arrange a meeting with Don at his next performance. The date came, Don's road manager had gotten us good seats and he came out before the show to meet me," said Michael.

"Wow," he said," You really have Don's look. After the show, stand over there and we'll take you back to meet him. What do you do for a living?"

"I'm a comedian, I do a tribute to Don," I said. He liked that, then walked away. Ten minutes later he was looking through the side curtains at me, waving. Standing next to him was Don, smiling and waving also! Backstage afterward, I met the great Don Rickles! He autographed a picture for me and I had a photo taken of us as I told him what an honor it was to meet him. He thanked me, then asked

'Do people tell you that you look like me?' 'Yes,' I said. 'Well, you're a good-looking guy!' cracked Rickles. Then I told his road manager, Tony, what an honor it was to meet *him* as he had been Frank Sinatra's manager for 15 years. 'And now you're stuck with Rickles??' I asked. 'Now that's funny,' laughed Don. I then asked his permission to do a tribute act to him. He said 'Yes, keep my name alive!'

And that's what I'm doing. Ya hockey puck."

"An 'insult comic' is the title I was given. What I do is exaggeration. I make fun of people, at life, of myself and my surroundings." —Don Rickles

Rhys Whittock

as Prince Harry

MANY AMERICANS ARE FASCINATED with the British Royal family and none more so than Prince Harry, the younger son of Charles, Prince of Wales, and Diana, Princess of Wales. In the past, Harry had a reputation as being somewhat randy although he tried to keep a low profile, as much as is possible for a direct descendant to the throne of England. However, when he married American actress Meghan Markle both were thrust into the worldwide spotlight. Their subsequent headline-making announcement in January of 2020 that they were stepping back from their role as senior members of the royal family only increased public curiosity and scrutiny.

Rhys Whittock and Sarah Mhlanga are lookalikes for Prince Harry and Meghan. Based in the UK, they are perfect examples of how the job of a lookalike mirrors that of the real celebrities. As Sarah points out, "When Meghan is busy, I'm also busy. As her fortunes rise and fall, so do my own. When Meghan is pregnant, I must also appear to be expecting. I had to wear a silicone 'baby bump' for numerous photo shoots and appearances." Rhys says his first diaper change happened on a photo shoot!

Rhys says that for him, "It all started years ago when a whole table of wedding guests began staring and smiling at me. My friend told me they were thinking I looked like Prince Harry! After receiving so many comments from the public in the street, I thought maybe there could be something more to this. My friends and family encouraged me to sign up with lookalike agencies. I applied to them but never received any response back. It was really Meghan Markle that catapulted me into this incredible industry so I have her to thank. The very next day after their huge engagement announcement in front of the world's press in 2017, I became a professional lookalike."

What happened? "Incredibly one of the agencies I applied to years ago had kept my details on file. They contacted me by email," he continued.

"Hey Rhys, I don't suppose you still look like Prince Harry, do you?" they wrote.

"I replied yes, went to their office and signed up right away!"

They explained that Harry, as a high-profile target, had received death threats during his time in the Army in Afghanistan and had kept quite a low media profile for security during his army years. Therefore, there had been little demand for Harry lookalikes but they could tell by the enormous media coverage of the engagement that lookalike work for Harry would soon come pouring in as this couple began to be featured on the front covers of every magazine across the world.

"One week before the wedding I won a competition with the British airline, EasyJet. They were searching for the best Harry and Meghan lookalikes in Europe. We received a royal carriage tour around Buckingham Palace and Westminster, dressed as if we just got married! I'll never forget the tourists with their smartphones capturing the moment. That was an incredible day. Plus, I also received free flights for a whole year!"

In 2019, with the arrival of Harry and Meghan's baby, Archie, they became busy with lots of photo shoots with babies, using dolls and real babies. Then with the huge news of their departure from the Royal family in January 2020, "we were unsure what this meant for work. If Harry and Meghan disappeared from the front pages, I thought work could possibly dry up. I needn't have worried as 'Megxit' proved to be good for business as Harry and Meghan got even more media coverage than ever before."

"Royalty is completely different than celebrity. Royalty has a magic all its own." —Phillip Treacy

129

SARAH IS A TRAINED ACTRESS, quite capable of playing many roles. She initially had mixed emotions about being "Meghan," much the same way other actors and actresses worry about becoming typecast as one character or one type of character. She was also concerned that some might not consider lookalike work to even be a worthy acting assignment. But competition in the creative arts is keen and the heart of acting is to realistically portray someone other than yourself.

Sarah didn't even realize that being a lookalike was a "thing" until people started telling her that she looked like Meghan, around the time of Prince Harry's engagement.

"I wasn't working all that much and my agent said, 'Why don't you try some lookalike work?' So, my first job as Meghan was at a Princess-themed birthday party for eight and nine year-old girls. As Meghan, I was teaching them 'princess etiquette,' such as how to hold one's teacup, how to get on and off the train delicately and more. It was quite fun and I rather enjoyed it," she says. "Now, I see it as just another role to play, perhaps one that draws on my improvisational skills more than a traditional theatrical project."

Certainly, the royal couple has had their ups and downs. Sarah says, "One minute, everyone loved Meghan, the next minute, everyone was upset with her. At one point, some were even criticizing her for cradling her 'baby bump' which I personally thought was tender and endearing. Public opinion goes up and down but when people found themselves unhappy with her, they would tell me! I found myself defending her at times, but at the same time I wondered why they were telling ME?"

This sort of thing happens to lookalikes and impersonators often. Perhaps it's a credit to their acting skills and believability that people feel they can vent to them as well as praise them. Rhys and Sarah are both grateful for the opportunities afforded them as the "royal couple" and since the real royal couple has relocated to California, there is a high probability that America may be seeing more of Rhys and Sarah!

"There's no more private family than the royal family. People who can really only be themselves with each other. The rest of us just spend all our time fascinated by them." —John Lithgow

130

Sarah Mhlanga
as Meghan Markle

Monica Leamy
as Gwen Stefani

"INITIALLY, WHEN I WAS VERY YOUNG, I was told that I resembled Gwen Stefani and Audrey Hepburn but I didn't know impersonation was a 'thing.' Unless you are part of that world, you don't really know or think about tribute bands, artists, corporate gigs, lookalikes, etcetera."

One of Monica's first jobs was as one of the 'Shagadelic girls' for an Austin Powers impersonator. "I learned and got experience. I had mentors. I played Audrey Hepburn, Marilyn Monroe, Katy Perry, Madonna, Debbie Harry from Blondie and others. One thing led to another and I found myself actually starting to make a living within this world of impersonation and tribute artists."

Monica says, "When I first started pursuing the character of Gwen Stefani, she was not all that popular because she was lying low, raising her kids and taking a bit of a hiatus. What helped was that she began appearing on a popular television show called *The Voice*. It also didn't hurt that she began dating – and eventually marrying - Blake Shelton, a country heartthrob who was also appearing on the show. When I met my husband, Jonathan, a musician, we started to put together the tribute band Subliminal Doubt, and the character of Gwen started taking off!"

Monica actually got to meet Gwen the first night of her honeymoon. "We went to Vegas and saw her show. I dressed as Gwen and made a poster because I know that Gwen tends to read them. In the middle of a song, she saw me and reacted. I thought maybe she would say hi or read my poster but she pulled me up on stage, telling the audience about me! She actually had me speak into her mic and she was so nice! It was incredible. I told my husband that the honeymoon couldn't possibly have gotten any better."

Monica says, "The best thing about my career is I get to pretend to be a rock star without the pressure of actually having to be one! It has definitely taken me places I would never have gotten to go otherwise and it has made me braver. Me as Monica never thought that I would be performing in front of 500 to 700 people. The worst thing about being a Tribute Artist is that I am completely at the mercy of the star that I portray so when they make changes in their music, their look, their personae, perhaps changes that I can't do or incorporate into my show, I'm stuck. I also have to hope that she doesn't do anything to get herself cancelled in the eyes of the world or fall from grace."

One of the hardest shows that Monica has ever done was a gig right after things began opening up after COVID in May 2020. It was supposed to be a virtual show but the venue was opened and operating at 25% capacity. Her father was super excited that he was going to get to finally see her show but sadly, the day before the show, he passed away. Monica was devastated. "We had to make all kinds of changes; my friends came and supported me and I got through the show. If he could have been there, I would have wanted to thank him for giving me a love of music and performing and making me feel that a career in the arts was completely valid." The show must go on.

"Music is the language of the spirit. It opens the secret of life bringing peace, abolishing strife." —Kahlil Gibran

Dan Schneid
as Dr. Phil

D AN WAS A HOME IMPROVEMENT STORE MANAGER in Laguna Niguel, CA but as more and more people came to know Dr. Phil McGraw from his hit television show, more and more people mistook Dan for the popular purveyor of advice. A David Letterman impersonator, Gregg Chelew, was shopping in the store one day and told him he looked like Dr. Phil. "Who?" said Dan, who had never watched the show and had never even heard of Dr. Phil back then. When he did catch the show, he was a bit taken aback that he looked so much like the straight-talking host and author.

Gregg pointed out the possibilities as well as some things he could do to enhance the resemblance, such as growing his mustache, his sideburns and more. Within two weeks, people were asking the cashiers at the store if Dr. Phil shopped there. On short notice, Gregg took Dan to a convention for celebrity impersonators in Las Vegas, advising him to bring business cards. Armed with 20 home-made business cards and bio sheets, which Dan had initially thought was overkill, they were gone within 20 minutes. He and Gregg performed a skit and Dan became Dr. Phil! "It was a very exciting and scary experience and yet I was drawn to it. Crazy as it seems, it was awesome to be him!!!" says Dan.

Like many true Lookalikes, sometimes Dan has trouble convincing people that he is NOT who they think he is.

"I was at a Convention for Celebrity Impersonators in Florida and after a great but long week, I was heading home to California. I took a late flight and arrived at John Wayne airport in Orange County at about 11 pm. I had parked on the top floor of the parking structure attached to the airport. As I got off the elevator and I'm walking down the very long walkway, I see a man in a very nice dress suit walking in my direction, about 10 feet to the right. All of a sudden, he veers right toward me. As he gets closer, I think that if he is going to mug me then he certainly got dressed up for the part. However, as he draws near, he says, 'May I approach?' Bewildered, I say yes. He put his hand out and says, 'I want to thank you for all you do and all the people you help, I love your show!"

Dan goes on to explain, "I'm in a pair of jeans, a T-shirt and a backward baseball cap, pulling my suitcase and I try to explain that I'm not who you think I am and he says, 'I know you have to say that, but I really like what you do to help people.' At this point, I'm tired and really trying to tell this guy I'm not him so I pull out my driver's license and show him. He 'snaps' it three or four times which is a trick to see if the laminate peels, indicating a possible fake ID. He realizes it is authentic and says, 'Wow, they even gave you a real fake driver's license, that's good!' I realize that I can't win so I tell him, 'Thank you, I appreciate you watching the show and will continue to do my best.' He shakes my hand, thanks me again, tells me to have a great night and walks away. I look up at the security camera, shrug my shoulders, smile and walk away. Sometimes it feels like I'm living in an alternate reality!"

Has he ever met the infamous Doctor Phil???

Dan and a girlfriend had gotten tickets to attend the Dr. Phil show, telling them in advance that he was a Dr. Phil impersonator. When they started to get in line for the show, it caused such a commotion that they were invited by security guards to come to the front of the line. They declined, saying they could stand in line like everyone else but as they again attempted to join the queue, a massive disruption occurred with fans screaming and hugging him. This is not an unusual situation for lookalikes and more than one lookalike has been asked to leave the premises because of the disturbance they cause, however unintentionally. A true lookalike often cannot lead a normal life in public without a bit of a disguise, like their famous counterparts.

Dan and his girlfriend were then escorted to a room near the studio and seated in a prime spot in the audience, who again assumed him to be the real deal. Dr. Phil spotted him during the taping but pro that he is, remained unfazed and focused on the issue at hand.

Afterwards, the executive producer asked them to come and meet the real Dr. Phil McGraw, who is a little bigger than Dan Schneid but that doesn't matter. The mustache, the tie, the lack of hair are all there as well as the candor and humor. Since then, he has been on the set two more times.

"I have received a lot of attention that was ... let's say, not asked for, but not refused. The fact that I wake up looking like him is crazy enough but when you're walking down the street and someone says, 'Hi, I love your show—may I have a picture with you?' How do you say no? You take the picture and let their dream continue."

Sometimes a fan, convinced that Dan is Phil, will get excited. Dan will sometimes wink and put his finger up to his lips, motioning for them to be quiet, like they are in on a secret. And their dream continues.

"How's that workin' for ya?" —Dr. Phil

Steve Edenbo
as Thomas Jefferson
Photo © Jeff Fusco

STEVE EDENBO HAS BEEN STUDYING AND portraying Thomas Jefferson since 1999. He has most often portrayed Jefferson in Independence National Historical Park and in venues like Independence Hall, The City Tavern, The Declaration House, The US National Archives in Washington DC, The University of Virginia, Monticello and many more. His most regular and longstanding client is American Historical Theatre, which is a nonprofit organization based in Philadelphia.

Playing a historical figure presents its own set of challenges and rewards. For instance, there are no movies or videos available to learn mannerisms, voice, etc. One has to rely on accounts and research from the annals of history for much of the information which shapes the performance. However, this can sometimes give way to a more truthful presentation and an even more intense understanding of the character.

"I was working as an actor in 1999 when I was first approached to portray Thomas Jefferson. It was a "meet & greet" appearance, which are almost entirely improvisational, based on prior research, but I had read only a couple of books on him before this first booking. Without a previous grounding in the history of America's founding era, two or three books on Jefferson is a good number to get you into trouble without getting you out. That first performance humbled and thrilled me. I fell in love with the combination of reading, writing, acting, teaching, and traveling that this profession promised."

Steve says his favorite part of studying and portraying Thomas Jefferson is the conversation, in its larger sense, that he is "privileged and challenged to nurture with many audiences. More than any of the other United States founders, Jefferson stands at the center of some of the most complicated debates and deeply-rooted contradictions that run through America's past and present. I am deeply humbled and honored by this responsibility."

The journey has not been easy.

"The first time I was booked to perform for the FBI, I was terrified, as one would be. They could ask me any questions they wished to ask. We were at Monticello, and they'd just spent the whole day touring the house and grounds. But they liked my performance so much that they invited me out for beer and fried chicken afterwards. They didn't have to do that. It was one of the sincerest and most welcome compliments I have ever received. I had a similar experience when I performed for three hours for an audience of over 300 judges."

Along the way, Steve has been able to meet some of his own favorite actors.

"Very early in my career I met Tom Selleck at a gig. He introduced himself and asked for my advice about preparing and researching to portray a real historical figure, which he was about to do for a mini- series. I was and am a big fan of his, so I was struggling not to just go full-on fanboy and ask for his autograph. I'd like to think that I said something intelligent about how the techniques of Konstantin Stanislavski and Uta Hagen complimented the study of the actual facts of an historical person's life for the development of a character. I may have approximated something like that, because I was certainly thinking it. Then again, I may have gibbered like a silly person, I was downright starstruck. Around the same time, I portrayed Jefferson in a documentary produced and directed by Richard Dreyfuss. I'm afraid I may not have been ideally cool and composed when I met him as well."

Any other notable appearances? "I appeared as Jefferson on the Colbert Report… with two other Jefferson's. The idea was that we were competing in a game of "America's Top Jefferson." Three and a half hours of filming resulted in about 3 minutes of actual video being broadcast on the show."

What is the most interesting thing people have said to him while in character?

"A few people have told that they believe I'm the actual reincarnation of Thomas Jefferson. They were 100% serious. I wasn't sure how to respond. Saying, "thank you" didn't seem quite right. I still wouldn't know how to respond to that."

Are there any downsides to portraying the American statesman who served as the third President of the United States?

"The worst part of studying and portraying Thomas Jefferson is the misinformation that is spread about him. False quotes and facts, or quotes and facts decontextualized in such a way as to indicate something quite different than he ever meant or did, are a source of many headaches for me. I continue to research Jefferson and his times. I continue to strive for better ways to engage Jefferson's legacy in a meaningful conversation with modern times. I continue to be amazed at what I did not know ten years ago. Likewise, I continue to be aware that I will know qualitatively more ten years from now. Jefferson had 83 years to learn about himself. It's pretty unlikely that I'll have as much time at the same puzzle. I'm happy to say, however, that I'm enjoying the process. More importantly, my audiences are enjoying the process, and that's the best I could hope for."

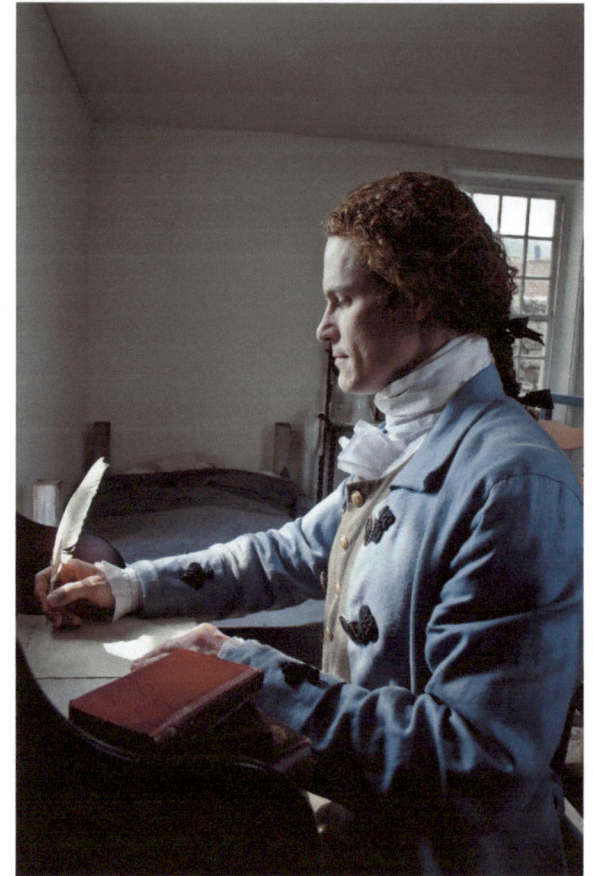

Photo © Karla Korn

"We might as well require a man to wear still the coat which fitted him when a boy, as civilized society to remain ever under the regimen of their barbarous ancestors." —Thomas Jefferson to Samuel Kercheval, 7.12.1816

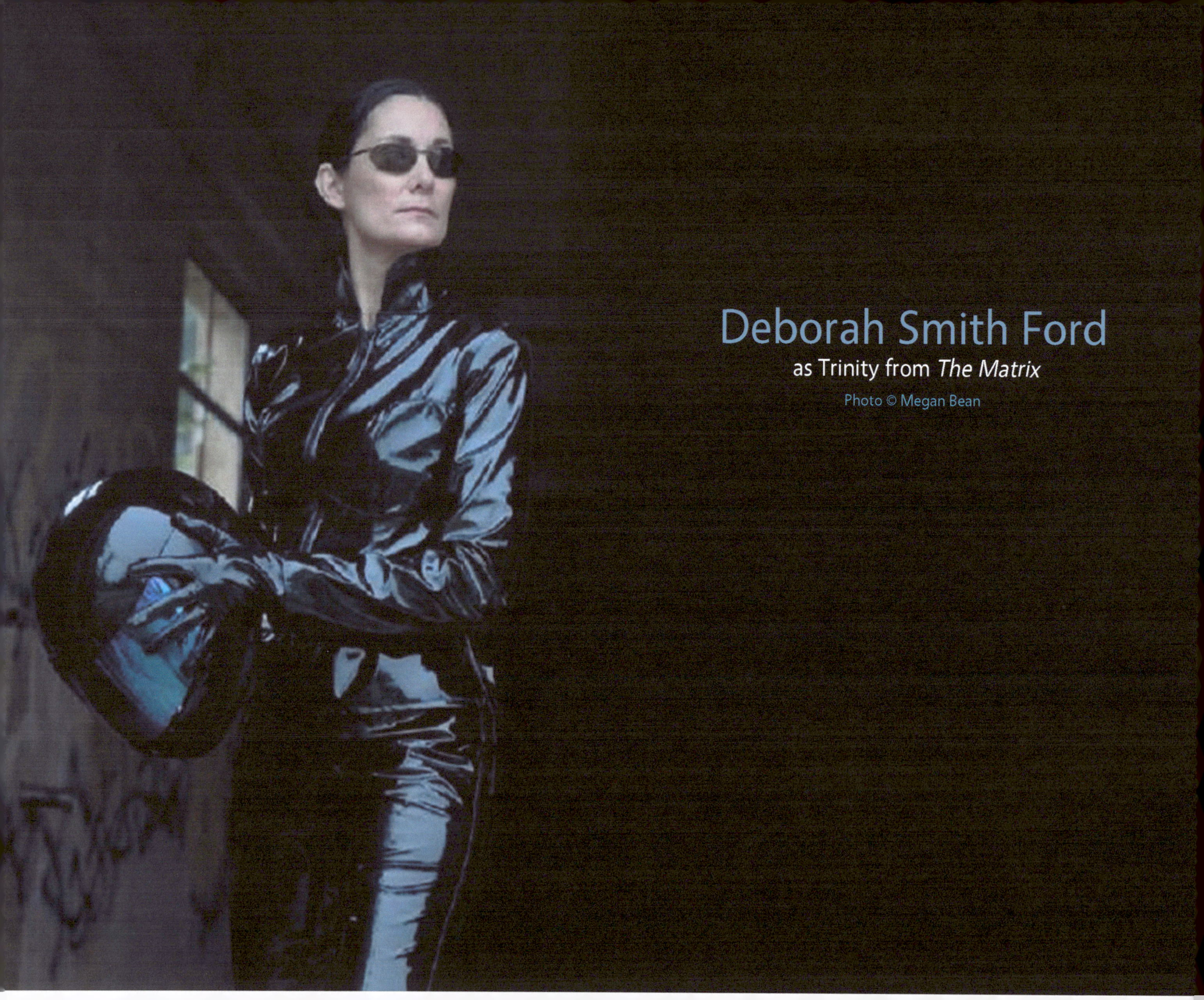

Deborah Smith Ford

as Trinity from *The Matrix*

Photo © Megan Bean

TRINITY IS A FICTIONAL CHARACTER PLAYED BY the actress Carrie-Anne Moss in the futuristic, sci-fi *Matrix* series. In the film, her character is well-known and somewhat legendary among computer hackers. She knows martial arts, is skilled with firearms as well as other weapons and can drive cars, motorcycles and even helicopters! This no-nonsense heroine seems completely at odds with Deborah Smith Ford, a wife, mother and grandmother. Ford has experience in teaching, modeling, dental and veterinary assisting and as a missionary. But therein lies the soul of a trained actress. Ford's acting and entertainment background is varied and diverse. She has portrayed different characters both as a lookalike and an actor. So is there a difference?

According to many sources, lookalikes and impersonators are truly consummate actors; they must be gifted in the art of improvisation because they are often hired for unscripted performances and appearances. They must know their character thoroughly and develop them independently. They must copy exactly the appearance, mannerisms and sometimes voice of the original or come as close as possible. This draws on the discipline of acting more than the creative aspect.

Ford says "When on a film or TV set, a variety of departments take care of the actors' needs but celebrity impersonators and lookalikes have to research, thus adapting techniques, methods, wardrobe…everything, all on their own!"

Ford is often asked about her technique, how she gets into character and which method(s) she prefers. "Whether I'm acting in film or television, or as a celebrity lookalike, I tend to use what works best in each scenario. Film and television scripts act as a major guideline, wardrobe and makeup certainly help, and the director or writer usually has a say as well. As a lookalike, it is similar but on the whole I feel I have more control. Sometimes improvisation works best for me both as an actor and a lookalike, although if other actors are involved then sticking to a script is often the best technique. When my lines and/or blocking (moves I make as the character) are firm in my head, and I'm in my wardrobe, then I am 99% in the mode, both as an actor and as a lookalike."

So why not 100%?

"For me as a performer, I have to allow at least 1% of me, as Deborah, to exist. That gives me better control. After all, these performances are pretend but my goal is to have the audience think, even for a short time, that what they are enjoying is real!"

Many lookalikes are asked, "How did you get in this business and why did you choose this particular character?" Ford comments: "Since I was/am an actress it was easy adding 'lookalike' to my repertoire, although in the early 2000s, I had no idea what the *Matrix* films were about. But multiple people asked me to pose for photos and sign autographs, thinking I was the actress in the original film. As a result, I have learned all things *Matrix*."

"In the movie trilogy, Trinity's wardrobe consists of shiny tight black pants, top, coat, boots, dark sunglasses and cool weapons of all kinds. I tend to downsize the 'firearms' when attending events, and it's easier getting on airplanes without them!"

143

Trinity is not the only character that Ford portrays as a lookalike. Some of her other looks include Miss Peregrine from *Miss Peregrine's Home for Peculiar Children*, TV's Sabrina from *Charlie's Angels*, Audrey Hepburn, the Queen of Narnia, plus Mary Katherine Gallagher from *Saturday Night Live* and *Superstar* but Trinity is, by far, her most popular look.

Ford is also a writer and has been featured inside and on the cover of the February 2020 issue of *Story Monsters Ink* magazine. She is the author of the Allie's Adventures Series, and these books, as seen through the eyes of a child, give readers of all ages a taste of what it's like in the worlds of entertainment, farming, travel and more.

"I'm a skilled professional actor. Whether or not I've any talent is beside the point." —Michael Caine

Photo © Israel David Groveman

Photo © Jeff Kaine

Caroline Bernstein
as Sharon Osbourne,
the Queen and
Margaret Thatcher

Photo © Caroline Bernstein

THE POSH, UPPER-CLASS ACCENT KNOWN AS the Queen's English comes very naturally to Caroline Bernstein as she has lived in the UK her entire life. She does vocal impressions of more than 20 celebrities with stunning accuracy. "It's an 'authentic' vocal impression of the Queen," says Caroline. She can also appear in person as the Queen along with Britain's former Prime Minister Margaret Thatcher and comedienne Joan Rivers. Her most popular character is Sharon Osbourne, television personality and wife of rocker Ozzy Osbourne from the band Black Sabbath.

Q. How and why did you get started in this business?

"I was trained as an actress and singer at *Italia Conti* drama school in the 1970's, then worked in theaters all over the United Kingdom in plays and musicals. I worked on several TV ad campaigns in the UK and Europe. I also performed as a stand-up comedienne on the cabaret circuit in London, a one-woman show at the Edinburgh Festival and became a host and after-dinner speaker for numerous blue-chip companies. While working as an actress portraying comedy characters in theater and children's television, I was offered the starring role of Margaret Thatcher in the theater production of *Anyone For Denis?*, a satirical play dealing with the domestic affairs of Britain's Prime Minister and her husband. I had always enjoyed doing vocal impressions so this gave me the opportunity to enter the world of celebrity impersonation."

Q. What do people say when they find out what you do?

"They are always fascinated and want to know if I've ever met the celebrities I impersonate. They always ask me to do the voices!"

Q. What characters do you do—and why those particular characters?

"I mainly work in the UK and some of my favorites are the Queen, Maggie Thatcher, Joan Rivers and the most popular has been Sharon Osbourne. As Sharon, I can 'glam up' a bit, with gorgeous outfits and sparkly jewelry! Sharon's voice is from London and she has a cute "girly" quality, it is quite shrill and innocent and I can get lots of comedy out of her delivery!! It's as if she's talking to a little puppy dog most of the time… I love doing her voice!! Why these characters? I've always loved performing strong women and comedy icons."

Q. Have you ever met any of them??

"Yes, I met Margaret Thatcher in the 1980s at her book signing, the Queen at one of her garden parties at Buckingham Palace, Joan Rivers at the Edinburgh Festival and Sharon Osbourne at the television studio while portraying her in an X-Factor sketch."

Q. Any particularly unusual or memorable gigs or experiences?

"One of the most memorable jobs was a few years back, in the South of France, where I was booked to play the very dignified and distinguished Prime Minister Margaret Thatcher as part of a huge celebration in a very beautiful hotel on the edge of the sea. I ended up dancing the Limbo on the beach in front of a huge cheering crowd shouting 'Go Maggie, Go!'"

Q. What is the funniest question or remark regarding your profession that you have ever received?

"I'm much younger, in real life, than the Queen, so at the launch of a shopping Center in Manchester, dressed as Her Highness, an audience member shouted out: "YOU DO LOOK WELL, YOUR HIGHNESS!" (I thought to myself, I should hope so. I'm 40 years younger.)"

Q. Have you noticed any differences between U.S. audiences and British audiences?

"The role of the celebrity impersonator is admired equally in the U.S. and in the U.K., but American audiences are definitely more responsive. They tend to 'let go' and are more generous with their reactions than the British."

Q. In your opinion, what's the best thing about being a celebrity impersonator or tribute artist?

"One of the best experiences over the years has been attending conventions for our industry in Las Vegas and Florida. I met many fellow tribute artists and impersonators who showed such support and generosity of spirit; we are all like one big family and many have remained dear friends over the years. People love to be entertained and uplifted and it's a blessing to be able to do that in this business. I'm doing the one thing I'm passionate about: performing comedy and entertaining people."

"The best and most beautiful things in the world cannot be seen or even touched—they must be felt with the heart."

—Helen Keller

Sean Banks

as President Barack Obama

"IN 2008, I WAS PLAYING MY GUITAR IN CHURCH when my trusted Telecaster suddenly died out on me. I wasn't able to finish the song but borrowed a guitar and finished playing the service, realizing that it was of utmost importance that I get my guitar fixed. Someone directed me to the Guitar Factory in Orlando. While there, I was surprised to see a photo of George W. Bush with a guitar. I said that I never knew that Bush played guitar and was shocked to find that he got it maintained there. The shop owner then informed me that the person in the photo was a man who impersonates the President of the United States and makes a lot of money doing so. I thought to myself, 'I wish I looked like the President. I'd go out on gigs, make serious money and have the time of my life.' Then I didn't think any more about it. Who would have thought the next President was going to look like me?"

Sean continues, "As time went on, shortly before President Obama took the Oath of Office, so many people mentioned the uncanny resemblance that I started to see it, too. Friends who lived in Key West invited us to stay with them for Fantasy Fest, an island-wide Halloween party. The theme that year centered around politicians. I figured I'd go as Obama and see if anyone there noticed the resemblance. I didn't even own a suit, flag pin or nice shoes at the time so I went to a Goodwill store, shelled out $4 and came away with a dark blue sport jacket. I found a piece of jewelry that my late mother-in-law had made resembling a flag and shined up my old shoes. Arriving in Key West, I donned the makeshift suit and went on a quest for conch fritters for lunch. Two people approached and said I had a 'good look.' I thought that was success and would have been ok with that. I had no idea what was about to happen when night fell."

Sean says that evening he expected to see "…a few short-skirted Sarah Palins and maybe a John McCain and a George Bush or two. I never thought that I would turn into the focal point of Duval Street. It got to the point where I couldn't walk 25 feet without crowds of people stopping me for photos. That night I learned how strong my wife was when women handed her their cameras and put their bare chests on me, smiling for a picture. I learned what it must feel like for Hollywood stars to deal with paparazzi. One thing led to another, then another. Next thing you know I'm sitting for professional photo shoots and have appointments with various agents."

One night, Sean was meeting with an agent who asked, "How much do you charge for your appearances?"

"I had no idea what to answer. What do I tell this guy… $10 bucks, $50 bucks? I don't know. I had never charged for this before. Then he informed me that he was planning on using my character for an appearance and asked if I'd be okay with $2500.00. "Well, yeah!" I replied.

People often ask if Sean has met Obama. "I haven't but not for lack of trying. As time went on, I shared the stage with other political impersonators, such as John Morgan as George Bush, Patsy Gilbert as Sarah Palin and the late Dale Leigh as President Clinton. One day we found ourselves at an appearance in Washington DC, where we rented a stretch limo, slapped the magnetic Presidential Seal on the sides and went joyriding before the gig. We decided to do an a cappella version of a performance we had put together. Right in front of the White House.

I thought that security would approach us, take us in and Obama would come and tell us not to do that anymore.

151

He said, "As we performed, a large crowd started to gather. Then, as if on cue, security came through the crowd. I thought, 'Here we go, they're about to haul us in.' But the security officers then lined up and waited for pictures with us. I couldn't believe it."

He recalls, "Throughout the years, I have done all different types of appearances from large corporate gatherings in convention halls, staying at 5-star hotels, riding in limos, using private dressing rooms and flying first class, to small gatherings with low budgets, staying in $47 hotels and finding makeshift dressing rooms. You haven't lived until you've done your make-up crouched behind a dirty 2003 Pontiac Sunfire in a hot, mosquito-infested garage."

He distinctly remembers an appearance in Sarasota, Florida. "We had no idea what to expect. As we pulled up in our 2000 Corolla, with 191,000 miles, peeling window film, plastic interior trim visibly hanging down and one remaining plastic hub cap, we noticed news cameras filming people arriving in Bentleys, Ferraris and stretch limos. My wife stopped well before we could be seen and had me get out and walk while she sped off and hid the car. The following week we had an appearance in Miami. We rented a Charger. For future engagements, we rented cars befitting of my character and I now own a Charger."

"What the people need is a way to make them smile…it ain't so hard to do if you know how."

—Doobie Brothers, Listen to the Music

Jeff Richards
as Tim McGraw

Photo © Michael Cairns

N HIS THIRTY-PLUS YEAR CAREER SO FAR, country artist Tim McGraw, with his trademark black cowboy hat, has released sixteen studio albums, ten of which have reached number one on the country album charts and one was designated as the top country album of 1994. He has won numerous awards and appeared in films. A tour with his wife, Faith Hill, a best-selling artist in her own right, is one of the highest-grossing tours in country music history. He has sold more than 80 million records worldwide, making him one of the best-selling music artists of all time.

Billy "Thunder" Mason was McGraw's drummer for over 18 years. It was he who started *The Ultimate McGraw Tribute Show* and chose Jeff Richards to play the part of Tim. Jeff now offers a tribute to the 1994 – 2011 era of Tim McGraw.

Q. How did you get into this business?

"I went to a Tim McGraw concert back in the 90's. He was fresh and new to the scene and a few people said that I looked like him. I started researching him and attending more concerts. I thought "I'm going to buy a black hat and see if I really could look like him." The more concerts I went to, the more it seemed that people saw a resemblance."

Q. Have you had anything done—any surgical procedures or other enhancements—to make yourself look like McGraw?

"I wear a black cowboy hat."

Q. Have you ever met the real Tim McGraw?

"Early on, I went to see him in Lake Tahoe and there weren't many people in the crowd. I told my friend I was going to go jump up onstage. Security threw me off, of course. But my friend somehow got us backstage passes where I got to meet Tim afterward. Nervous, I blurted out, "You're my biggest fan!"

"I'm your biggest fan?" said Tim. I got pictures with him then.

"Later, Tim was playing in Vegas. I was having some adult beverages and walking toward the stage when he pulled me up on stage with him! Then in 2016, in Tampa, Florida, at a concert, I was standing right by the stage and Tim pulled me up there again. This time, I actually got to sing with him. He gave me a hug and a handshake. That was super cool!"

Q. Any early mentors?

"A guy named Robert, from a band called the California Cowboys, had told me I looked like Tim. 'Learn some of his songs and we'll get you up to sing with us,' he said. After about six months, I ran into that band again. I had learned about two songs and this was the first time I had ever sung any Tim McGraw tunes. Robert was encouraging but he also told me I would need 'thick skin because people aren't always gonna be nice. They may try to provoke or insult you but you have to let it roll off your back. It won't always be smooth sailing.' And he was right."

Q. How so?

"Well, in different ways. At a Tim Show/concert I was attending, I was surrounded by people wanting autographs and pictures of me. One lady in particular kept asking why was I trying to pass myself off as Tim McGraw and making a big fuss, accusing me of trying to fool people! The crowd grew so large that security thought there was a fight, so they came over - and escorted me out. They said I was disrupting the concert. But it wasn't me – it was everybody else. Then on the way out, the lady who had made such a big deal and caused the most commotion had the nerve to ask for a picture and autograph! Also, Tim has a fan page on social media. Recently, I posted an old picture of myself and Tim from back in '97, as others were doing. Before I knew it, people were writing in comments like 'Why don't you be your own person instead of copying him? Why do you have to try to look like somebody else?' And so on and so forth…."

Jeff continues, "I don't have to try. This is just what I look like. Some people call it a curse, others call it a gift to look like a famous, talented person. I choose to look at the positive side; it's an honor to look like and represent Tim McGraw. In private, after shows, I try to keep a low profile and be true to myself as well as the character I play. After shows, we meet the crowd and take pictures. We listen to the show and see where we can improve. When I'm in character; I respect the character. Once that black hat goes on, I'm Tim McGraw for the audience. I try to stay as close to the character as possible. But I'm still me. It's just that others see Tim."

Q. Any particularly memorable gigs, fans or moments?

"Well, one lady used to bake cookies for us all the time! We really enjoyed that. Oh, at an outdoor concert in Nevada, this guy wanted an autograph and photo. Afterward, he kept repeating to friends, 'That REALLY was Tim McGraw that signed my momma's picture, man, that was really him…he's just a down-to-earth guy…what a super guy," as he waited in line to use the porta potties. Just then, I came along and ducked into one of the outdoor toilets and the guy got even more excited! 'See, he's just a normal guy—like us—just a regular guy! He even uses the porta potty!'"

Q. How has this job affected your life, if it has?

"It hasn't really affected ME, I'm still the same me but it has opened my eyes. I would never have gotten to travel across the United States. Never would have gotten to meet the people I have met, like Merle Haggard, for one. I never would have gotten to meet Tim McGraw probably! I just try to stay humble and I've never thought I WAS Tim McGraw."

One of the things Jeff likes best about being a Tim McGraw tribute artist is the joy he can bring to others. "People get into it and have a good time. I enjoy bringing Tim's music to people who can't afford to go or can't get to a Tim McGraw concert for any reason. I have performed at long-term care facilities and they really appreciate it. One lady was tapping her foot, smiling and clapping. The staff said they had never seen her like that; she was considered to be the 'meanest' person there, but for at least that one hour, she enjoyed herself. It warms your heart."

"A great song should lift your heart, warm the soul and make you feel good." —Colbie Caillat

Mark Staggs

as Festus from
the television series *Gunsmoke*

OLD-TIMERS WILL REMEMBER Marshall Matt Dillon, Doc and Miss Kitty from the popular television western *Gunsmoke* which ran for 20 seasons beginning in 1955. One of the most popular characters was 'Festus Haggen' as played by Ken Curtis. 'Festus' was a scruffy Tennessee mountain man of questionable repute, who had drifted in and out of Dodge for a while and may or may not, at times, have even been on the wrong side of the law. He was cantankerous, uneducated and wily, however, he joins forces with Matt as an official Deputy. His wry humor and cock-eyed countenance offered comic relief for the series.

Mark Staggs offers his own cock-eyed comic relief as a modern-day Festus. He can do other characters, including Peter Falk, Sylvester Stallone, Arnold Schwarzenegger, John Wayne, and more but Festus is his favorite.

"He is, by far, the most popular character that I do. I have made a career of impersonating him and doing standup comedy as Festus. I started doing the character when I met Ken Curtis at a rodeo in Yuma, Arizona while in the Marine Corps. He entertained for the county rodeo. I could already imitate him and when I lined up to get his autograph, I did my 'Festus voice' for him. He didn't care for it but everybody else in line thought it was great."

Mark says he wanted to be a movie star from the time he was five and would imitate the characters he saw on TV; their actions, the way they walked, etc. "But living in Texas in the 60's, opportunities were non-existent. In the mid 60's my dad bought a Bill Cosby album and I listened to it over and over. I had also seen Cosby doing his standup act on TV several times. Since I had memorized his stories and could imitate his hand movements and facial expressions, I started making people laugh, entertaining them and I became addicted!"

In the next year or so, he and his neighborhood gang went to the movie theater and watched *The War Wagon* with John Wayne. "When we came out, I impersonated Wayne for the guys - they were amazed. I became very popular for my impersonation of the Duke. I learned to do a few more impersonations while still in school but when I joined the Marine Corps, I found I could do almost any celebrity I wanted to. It came easy."

Mark continues, "Then came social media! I started doing impersonations on Facebook and YouTube. Around the same time, I had an opportunity to do my comedy for a cowboy church, so I decided to do it as Festus. People started hiring me to do more comedy as Festus and to just show up at their events in character. This was in 2015 and the gigs keep coming. I didn't know how popular and beloved this character was until then."

One show that stands out for Mark was emceeing the *Silver Spur Awards* that celebrate and recognize the actors and actresses who appeared in old cowboy and western movies. "It's a gathering for them to get together and talk about old times and share stories from the productions. I grew up watching these films and I got to meet many of the stars. My fondest memory was meeting Patrick Wayne (John's son) and Stephanie Powers, because my favorite John Wayne movie is *McClintock* in which they both appeared.""

159

Mark had only been doing the 'Festus Comedy Show' for a couple of years when he won Funniest Male and Most Unique Act awards at the *Sunburst Convention for Celebrity Impersonators* in Orlando, Florida.

'Doc' Adams: I'll tell you why the Hagens live so long.

Festus Haggen: Why?

'Doc' Adams: 'Cause they're too dumb to know they're dead! – from 'Gunsmoke'

Photo © Gary Barger

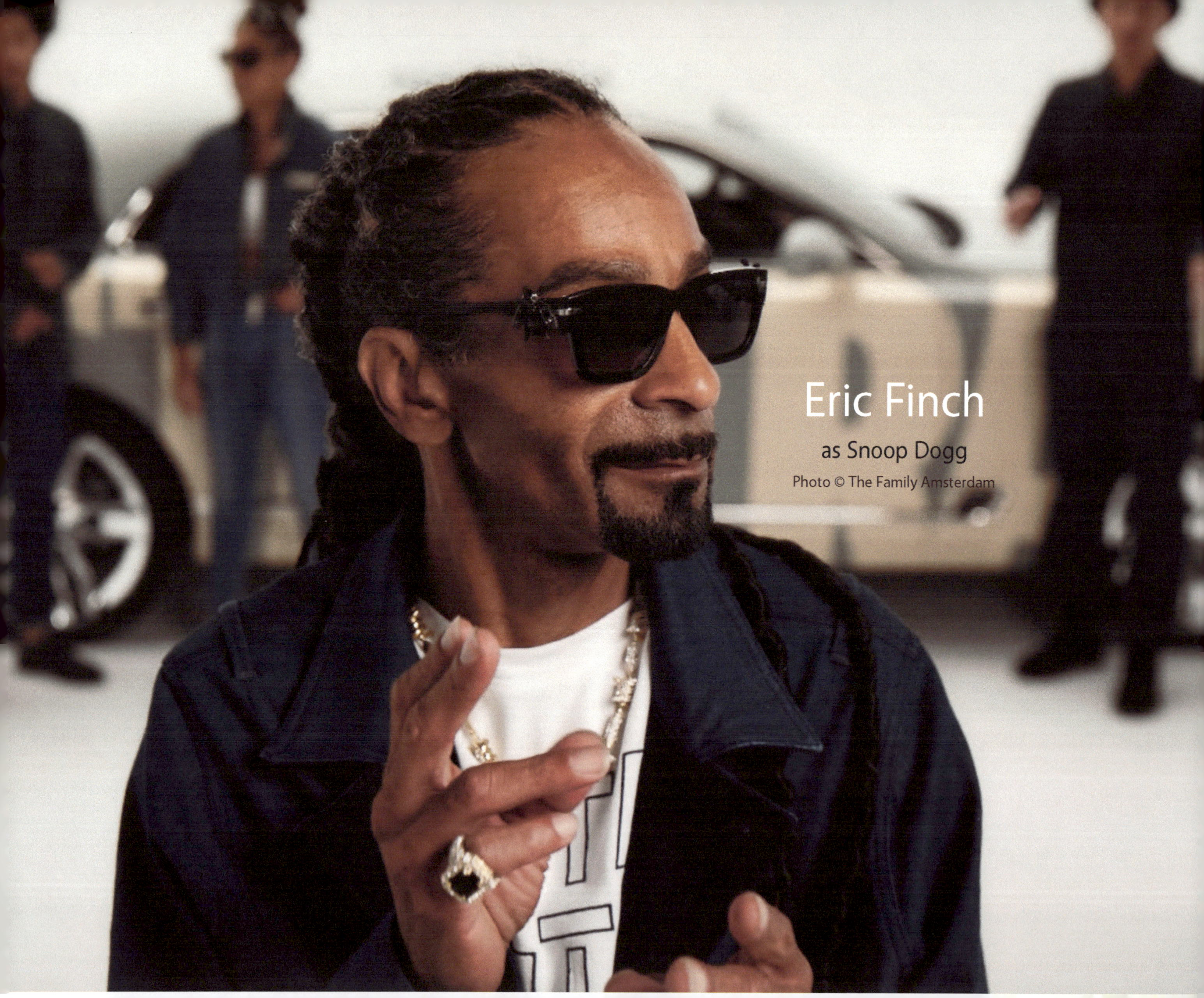

Eric Finch

as Snoop Dogg

Photo © The Family Amsterdam

ERIC FINCH, FROM LAKE CHARLES, LOUISIANA, enlisted in the Navy in 1988, and was stationed in the Philippines, then Camp Pendleton, California. When he finished his tour of duty from the armed forces, he began his career in show business as a Talent Relations Manager in one of the top clubs in Orange County. Working with Jamie Fox and rap artists such as Ludacris, Lil Jon, B.O.B. and top DJs Sander Van Dorn, Power 106, DJ Reflex and many others added to his entertainment background. He rapped with Southland Gangsters who went on to cut a CD and music video. Eric went on to become the top Snoop Dogg lookalike talent in the world. His résumé spans National/International TV shows, commercials, double/stand-in, voice over artist, documentaries and more.

Q. What's it like to work with the celebrity you portray?

"A dream come true—to be recognized by a peer who invites you into their world."

Q. How and why did you get started in this business?

"For several years while in the navy, my buddies would tell me I look just like Snoop Dogg. The funny thing is that I did not know who Snoop was but in 2013, I launched my career as a Snoop Dogg lookalike and reached out to several agencies. I haven't looked back since."

Q. Any particularly unusual or memorable gigs or experiences?

"I have had many memorable gigs. I was lucky enough to travel to Spain this year and work with an incredible production team from Holland and a local crew from Barcelona. Working on a commercial as a double is an exceptional experience."

Q. Any particularly memorable or unusual situations or fans?

"We were on location in LA. At the hotel we were staying at, a woman approached me to take a photo. The next thing I know, the photo had gone viral. The fan's son was a well-known internet blogger and he posted "How do I tell my mom that was not the real Snoop?'"

Q. Have you learned anything from doing this gig?

"Every day you learn something new on the set, in the studio or in live corporate appearances. But I have to say patience and respect are the biggest things you need to survive."

Q. How has this affected your life, if it has?

"It's been challenging—looking like a very famous person has its up and downs but it's a choice we make, to be in this niche of the entertainment industry. People I meet out and about sometimes don't believe me when I tell them I'm not the real Snoop. They think I am just saying that. So I smile and take the photo with them...."

Q. In your opinion, what is the best thing about being a celebrity impersonator/tribute artist?

"Bringing happiness and smiles to fans and exceeding client expectations."

Q. What is the worst thing?

"It's not really the worst thing, but it has taken the entertainment industry a long time to recognize that lookalikes are a specialized set of professional actors."

Q. What is the stupidest question or remark regarding your profession that you have ever gotten?

"That's easy; 'How long does it take you to look like Snoop Dogg?' My answer: Ask my mom & dad, LOL…"

"If it's flipping hamburgers at McDonald's, be the best hamburger flipper in the world. Whatever it is you do you have to master your craft." —Snoop Dogg

Sharon Holmes
as Martha Stewart
Photo © Doug Dobransky

MARTHA STEWART IS AN AMERICAN TELEVISION PERSONALITY, author and media mogul whose iconic empire was founded on cooking, hosting, decorating, gardening and all things domestic.

Sharon Holmes had often been told she looked like Martha. When she came across a Martha look-alike contest on the domestic diva's website while looking for a recipe, she sent in six pictures and stories about occasions when people thought she was Martha.

"In March of 2007, I received a call from one of the producers asking if I would come to New York and be on the show. At first, I thought it was a joke but then realized that this was the real thing. It isn't often that lookalikes get to meet the person they resemble, much less get invited to be on their show! It all happened very quickly. They flew me to New York on March 26th and we taped on the 27th," said Holmes.

While in New York, Stewart's stylist, Eva Scrivo did Holmes' makeup and hair.

"When I returned from the Salon about noon, the line was already forming for the 2 p.m. show taping. As I stepped out of the car, people at the end of the line saw me and started yelling 'Martha, Martha, we love you, we love your show!' I just waved and smiled. When we got back to the producer's office, word had already reached him that the studio audience had gotten all excited when they saw me. Things couldn't have gone better! As we walked upstairs, past people waiting to see the show, some started yelling again, 'Martha, we love you,' Holmes recalled. Later, the producer told Ms. Stewart that Sharon had fooled the entire studio audience.

Sharon says about her experience, "While I was in the studio offices, several members of Martha's personal staff walked by saying 'Morning, Martha!' We all got a good laugh. Patti LaBelle was a guest on the show that day. When she saw me sitting in the office, she waved and said 'Hi!' One of the staff said, 'Look! Patti thought she was Martha!' We had another laugh!"

According to Sharon, all of the people that she worked with were wonderful. Besides Eva Scrivo, Sharon had the opportunity to work with Mary Forest, one of the show's producers, the comedian Joey Kola and Wes, their head chef.

"Now I am Martha for trade shows, marketing events, corporate functions, award ceremonies, presentations, parties or any special occasion and as Martha always says, "That is a good thing!"

"So the pie isn't perfect? Cut it into wedges. Stay in control, and never panic." —Martha Stewart

Al Smith Jr.

as Tiger Woods

Photos © Michael Cairns

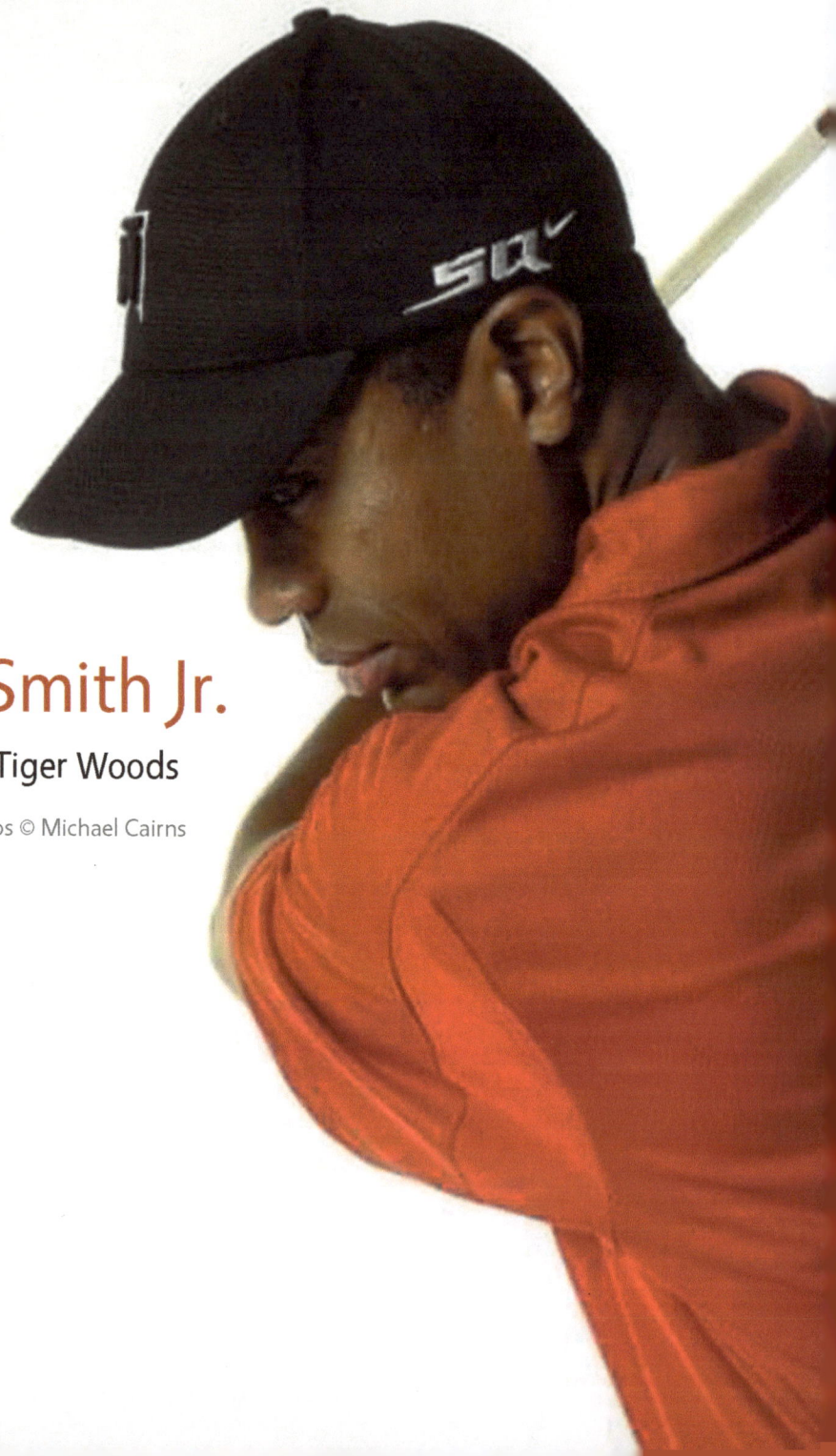

AL SMITH JR. GREW UP IN LOS ANGELES, California, Culver City, to be exact, which is steeped in movie-making history and known for its amazing talent pool of Hollywood actors.

"Bob Cosby (bother of comedian/actor Bill Cosby) was one of my early teachers. He along with my godbrother, Ted Lange, who played Isaac on the TV series *The Love Boat*, directed me towards acting, stand-in work and commercials so I had a little experience. As far as getting into impersonator/lookalike work, I kept hearing 'Has anyone ever told you that you look like Tiger Woods?' Especially when wearing a golf polo and cap. And I do play golf, quite a bit in fact."

He continues, "After hearing this for a few years, my good friend was picking up her dog from the dog-sitter and noticed a photo of what appeared to be President George Bush and his wife. She asked 'Is that you and the President?' The lady replied 'No, that's my husband. He is a celebrity impersonator. He impersonates President Bush.' It was John Morgan. My friend told the lady about me – that I looked like the famous golfer Tiger Woods. They had a discussion about the professional lookalike/impersonator industry and the lady offered contact information regarding conventions and people to speak with in order to learn more."

About 8 months later, Al reached out to the contact, who was informative and helpful. "He advised me to get some headshots and come to the convention that was taking place in about 3 weeks in Orlando. This was when I began taking things more seriously."

Al says, "I also deal in luxury automobiles and since then, my sales team entourage and I have had lots of opportunities to travel and golf at world class locations and to meet people and create friendships that will last a lifetime! We've also been chased out of malls, restaurants, and hotels around the country by friendly fans. One time, we were in the lobby checking in to The Ameri-Star Casino in Kansas City, Missouri when another patron spotted me. When I went up to my room he inquired as to whether it was actually Tiger Woods that he had just seen. My guys - always on point - proceeded to have a little fun and implied that it was, but that I was not in the best of moods after a bad showing at The British Open and I probably wouldn't be coming down for a bit. Forty-Five minutes later the gentleman was still waiting in the lobby, paper and pen in hand hoping to get a glimpse and autograph."

Has he ever met the real Tiger Woods? "I met Tiger very briefly in passing at one of the local sports restaurants in Orlando. I have also been fortunate enough to see him play at quite a few PGA Events and his former swing coach Sean Foley is one of our luxury automobile clients. I think if I were able to ask Tiger a few questions, I would ask him how he manages the pressure so well and what tip would improve my game the best?"

How close is the resemblance? "Well, while driving in Orlando with my parents, my mother noticed a billboard advertising TAG Heuer luxury watches and asked me, 'When did you shoot the photo for that?' I had to tell her that it was Tiger and not me!"

Al says that being a Tiger Woods impersonator has been a blessing in his life and he always tries to portray him in the best light possible. "He is the only celebrity that I impersonate and hopefully I can honor the opportunity as long as I am able."

"Golf is a fascinating game. It has taken me nearly 40 years to discover that I can't play it." —Ted Ray

BRITNEY SPEARS, SOMETIMES REFERRED TO AS the "Princess of Pop," is one of the best-selling artists of all time. She was groomed to be an entertainer from a very early age with dance lessons, gymnastics, voice lessons and singing in the church choir in Kentwood, Louisiana. She performed on the Mickey Mouse Club along with Christina Aguilera, Justin Timberlake, Ryan Gosling, and Keri Russell from 1992 to 1994 and has broken all sorts of records for recording artists. In the U.S. alone, she has sold more than 70 million albums, singles and songs. Britney names Madonna and Janet Jackson as major influences and inspiration for her dance-heavy style. Her personal life has had some turbulence but she is an enormously successful and talented entertainer.

Ashley Pitzer has wanted to be a performer since she was 8 years old. She worked at it, won a few dance competitions and realized she wanted to stand out and do more. From there, she dropped out of college, quit her job at a bank and began life as a Britney Spears tribute artist.

Her show is called *Britney One More Time*.

Q. Why Britney Spears?

"I felt that I really resonated with her, others said there was a resemblance and a sort of 'shared spirit.' It felt very natural."

Q. Britney names Madonna and Janet Jackson, among others, as influencing her dance-heavy style. Who are some of your influences besides Britney?

"My major influences would be Janet Jackson, Michael Jackson, Lady Gaga and Dolly Parton!"

Q. What is the best part and worst part about being a Britney Spears Tribute Artist?

"The best part? I think getting to meet Britney's fans, because I'm a fan, too! Also, all the amazing opportunities that have come my way. The worst part? Being an entertainer is tough sometimes. The entertainer lifestyle is no picnic and it's a lot of work. I'm a mother of a young child and it's sometimes difficult balancing all that."

Q. What do you mean by the 'entertainer lifestyle?'

"The late nights, the physicality, the mental preparation of getting into character and attention to detail, the pressure to be always 'on.' Mostly pressure from other people's expectations. Sometimes it's hard for people to accept me when I'm not in 'Britney mode.' At times, in social settings, they expect to see Britney but I'm NOT Britney and I know myself very well."

Q. How do you handle this?

"Sometimes, I need to be able to step outside myself and take an honest look. I conscientiously try to be aware of my independence from Britney—we are two different people."

Q. What do you do or have you done in order to look like Britney?

"I have never had cosmetic surgery or altered my face to look like Britney Spears but I have colored my hair monthly, I do wear brown contacts and I work out five days a week with a trainer! I also highlight my face to match the shape of her face!"

Q. What is the stupidest question or remark regarding your profession that you have ever gotten?

"A lot of people assume I don't love myself or don't like who I am because I play a character for a living."

Q. That seems to be a misconception that is more common than one would think within the Tribute Artist/Impersonator community—or that Tribute Artists don't have a life of their own—or the performers think they ARE the person they impersonate. Nothing could be further from the truth with the bona fide professionals. Have you learned anything from playing Britney?

"Britney has taught me so much! The biggest lesson I learned from her currently is how strong I can be for myself and I can face any hurdles that come my way."

That would be a good thing for anyone to know.

"Bottom line: If you love yourself, it will all work out." —Britney Spears

Keith George

as Boy George

A S TIME MARCHES ON, EACH DECADE BRINGS new challenges, new norms, new heroes and villains. Occasionally, there is a resurgence of interest and nostalgia for a specific period in history and one may find an occasional roaring 20s party, a 1950s sock hop or a trend toward 1970s bohemian chic hippie styles. Currently there seems to be a fascination with all things from the 1980s and 90s.

The flamboyant, affable and imitable Boy George, born George Alan O'Dowd in Eltham, South London, England, was not only a musical influence but a cultural icon of the times and has remained active in entertainment circles well into the new millennium. With his androgynous, theatrical appearance and soulful voice, he easily became a familiar figure within the New Romantic Movement that began to emerge in the UK in the early 80s. His biggest successes in America were with the band Culture Club but he has gone on to do solo work as well.

UK based Keith George possesses the same kind of ambiguous sexuality and charisma as Boy George. He also possesses copies of the outrageous outfits and bears more than a passing resemblance to the original Boy George.

Q. So, how did you get into this line of work?

According to Keith, "I've been singing all my life, in school and such but after I became legal at age 18, I began singing in a local pub—nothing special really, the sort of place where one might stop in after work…"

A guy in the pub heard Keith's soulful, sweet voice and told him he sounded like Boy George.

"But I wasn't even singing a Culture Club song. I was singing reggae—Bob Marley tunes." says Keith.

Then the guy told me, "There's going to be a talent competition in a couple of weeks. I'll bet you would win it if you sang a Boy George song and dressed up like him."

I replied, "Oh, I couldn't… wouldn't do that, that's just not me…I don't want to do that..." He said, "Well, the prize is £2,500 (or $5,000 in US dollars at the time)."

Quickly I said, "Put my name down!"

"So in 1990, I won the grand prize money plus a management contract as a Tribute artist."

Q. Have you ever met Boy George personally?

"We are friends now but I first actually met him in 1996, in London and he wasn't aware of what I was doing at that point. We became friends in 2000, in Sydney Australia. I was doing some shows there. He was on a world tour with Culture Club and was in Sydney for one night. I got to go to the concert because one of my friends was a backup singer for him. We went backstage afterward and he said to me 'You look very familiar!'

175

I said, 'Yes, well, I'm Keith George and I impersonate you with the Boy George Experience.'

He said, 'Oh, yes! I like you—I like what you do!' It was an amazing moment and from then on we've become very close. He's one of my best friends."

Q. Have you ever had a 'wardrobe malfunction?'

"Some of my outfits have Velcro closures because of quick costume changes and on one occasion I was dancing around onstage, not realizing that the Velcro at the top of my trousers had come loose and my trousers fell down. It was truly a show-stopper! I told people that they *really* were getting the Boy George experience."

Q. What are some of the drawbacks in this business, besides the occasional wardrobe malfunction?

"One of the hardest parts is that it can be very lonely. In doing shows, there is a natural 'high' onstage. But then you come offstage and head for the dressing room alone and it's a bit of a letdown, especially on the drive home but many entertainers experience this. Also, when you get the occasional heckler or critic. You can do a show with a hundred happy, adoring fans and have one who criticizes you, and that's the one you will focus on and dwell on; the one negative person. I understand most entertainers go through this as well!"

Q. You have been a successful Tribute Artist for quite some time now. What do you like best about this business?

"It is a community of entertainers, very loyal, very hard working and it can be very lucrative. You must study, put in the hours, spend the money to perfect the look and learn the character in order to be good at this. When I'm dressed as Boy George, I am treated as Boy George. The best part is that I can go onstage to an already-receptive audience who WANTS to see the character I portray. It is a ready-made audience! And by far, the most rewarding thing to me is Boy George's approval, him saying to me 'You do me proud.' His acceptance and support means the world to me."

"There's no better time than now to be who you are." —Boy George

Michael Firestone

as Michael Jackson

Photos © John Warfield

MICHAEL FIRESTONE IS ONE OF THE MOST well-known, talented and respected Michael Jackson tribute artists in the world. At age fourteen, he had his life planned out: he was going to be a rock star or Plan B was to become a Michael Jackson impersonator, in spite of the fact that he doesn't really resemble the king of pop music. Firestone is gifted enough with make-up, hair, costuming, voice, dance and some say the spirit of Jackson; it works.

Q. How and why did you get started in this business?

"At sixteen, I had a recording contract as myself but the company took 50% of everything, from stickers to concert proceeds to photos or anything I made money on as Michael Firestone and they wanted to keep all the masters (original recordings) of my own music. It was a five-year contract with a sunset clause for another two years. The company basically owned me. When I realized what I had gotten into, the only avenue open where they couldn't take 50% of me was as a tribute artist."

Q. Do you do other characters? Do you play any instruments? What was your first job as MJ?

"I only do Michael Jackson and I play guitar. I've been doing Michael now for over 20 years. It's been a crazy career - I love the fans; but don't care for some of the people on the business side. My first job was working for Jon Stewart's *Legends in Concert* Corporate."

Q. What are/were some of the biggest challenges in becoming the King of Pop?

"The make-up! I had the singing and dancing down already. I'm an artist and applied my art background to the make-up but it still took about three years for me to really get it right. The drag queens helped me a lot with that; you could be a dude looking like you just came in from cutting the grass and come out looking like Madonna. They were great—and very honest. I don't look like Michael. People have said that I look more like Criss Angel, the magician."

Q. Did you ever meet Michael Jackson?

"My wife and I had driven from North Carolina to Vegas. We walked into Caesar's Palace and there's a huge crowd there. Michael Jackson is shopping! My wife yelled, "MICHAEL FIRESTONE IS HERE!" He walks through the crowd. Security asks if I have a weapon. Then he just walked up to me and started talking. About a week or two later, he called and we talked for about eight hours. In person, that guy was beautiful, everything about him was perfect."

Q. Any particularly unusual or memorable gigs or experiences?

"I'm looking to get into TV possibly in the future. Japan has some of the best audiences; they go nuts. And Orange County fair is one of my favorites! They sing along to every word of every song."

Q. Funniest moments? Wardrobe malfunctions? Backstage antics?

179

"Well, it seems my zippers are always a problem! One night I had on red underwear, my zipper wasn't secured and some lady called me Magic Mike! Sometimes I have a lot of fun with NOT looking like Michael Jackson, when people don't know me. For instance, when I come on the stage or back stage before a show with no make-up, not in costume, no one would ever guess who I am, including the sound and guitar techs. Sometimes, I just tell people I'm a sound/guitar tech. Anyway, one night, before the show, the sound guy and I had a conversation about the movie *Goonies*, which we both loved. He showed me a *Goonies* tattoo he had. I could tell that he had no idea who I was but then I came out later, after the transformation and did the show. After the show, as Michael, I went over and told him I was going to watch *Goonies* that night and maybe get a tattoo, too! He just looked shocked. His eyes got real big and he was speechless!"

Q. What would you have been if not an entertainer?

"I would have been an artist of some sort; something creative or possibly gone into the military. My pop kind of wanted me to follow in his footsteps and he was in the Air Force. We lived on Air Force bases which was really kind of cool because to this day, if a jet flies over me, I can tell you what it is, the numbers, the kind of aircraft and everything about it!"

Q. What is the worst thing about this business?

"Putting on the make-up. Getting everything right. I listen to people. Fans can be brutal. One night I heard someone say, 'His sideburns are out of control.' So I fixed them the next night. I also hate dating. Dating is crazy because out of costume, it's great; they don't even know who you are. But you have to tell them sometime. Then they either don't like entertainers or they are big Michael fans and become obsessed. But my own problems disappear when I become Michael."

Q. In your opinion, what is the best thing about being a celebrity impersonator/tribute artist?

"I like to remind people that Michael Jackson is the greatest entertainer of all. No one comes close. In the past, sometimes people didn't necessarily like MJ or 'get him,' but I have had people come up and tell me that they were sorry that they didn't watch him when he was here but they are now a fan. I know MJ fans because I am the biggest one in the world! Their lives are enriched. And you just can't be in a bad mood when his music is playing. Michael Jackson was born to do this. I'm just a copy."

Firestone may be a white boy from Cleveland but onstage, he transcends color. And everything else.
Once in Chicago on a street corner after a show, a black woman pulled up in a car and asked him "Are you Michael Firestone?" He answered "Yes, Ma'am, I am." She said, "I love you." Michael Jackson would probably have loved it.

"Now I believe in miracles
And a miracle has happened tonight
But, if you're thinkin' about my baby
It don't matter if you're black or white."

—Michael Jackson, Black or White

In Memoriam

THE ADVENT OF AN INTERNATIONAL PANDEMIC took its toll on the entertainment industry as a whole. Some say that even if one didn't contract COVID, the stress of living in such a crazy time was enough to cause illness and death. Within the impersonator/tribute artist world, we have lost some of the best and brightest, from performers to agents. There may be others who are not listed here but to all, we would like to offer not just our condolences, but to express our sincere gratitude for the good times, talent and friendship shared. May you be at peace.

MARCEL FORESTIERI (November 21, 1953 – Sept. 18, 2021)

Marcel Forestieri was a one-of-a-kind performer, singer, actor, and impersonator. He started his career on Broadway as Conrad Birdie in *Bring Back Birdie.* He was one of the first official Elvis impersonators in the show *Little El.* He went on to become the number one Jay Leno impersonator in the world, making many appearances on the *Tonight Show* and the *Legends in Concert* series. He was always working and developing new shows and impressions including Regis Philbin, Wolfman Jack and Donald Trump. Marcel was a consummate professional and will be missed by the entire entertainment industry.

—John Di Domenico, Professional actor, writer and comedian

DALE LEIGH (January 19, 1956 – June 27, 2021)

I once told Dale, "You're the brother I never had." He retorted, "You're the brother I never wanted." We both laughed till tears ran down our cheeks. Laughing was a continuous part of Dale's relationships. He would always encourage me in some way and made a warm and lasting impression on everyone he met. A caring and thoughtful individual, Dale never missed a chance to ask how you were doing and then, really listen as you answered. He was funny, likeable and a priceless friend to me, a gifted musician and vocalist, a firebrand of opinion online, and had deep Christian faith and convictions. Albeit reluctantly at first, he became a gifted and capable Bill Clinton impersonator/comedian. He even landed a role playing Clinton in the movie *Definitely Maybe*, starring Ryan Reynolds. I impersonate George Bush and as two former Presidents, we traveled together often, performing the musical comedy show we created, "Bill and George's Excellent Adventure." Rest in Peace, Dale.

—John Morgan, Professional speaker, author, actor, and comedian

PETER ALDEN (July 17, 1966 – September 25, 2021)

This picture was taken several years ago at The Sunburst Convention. It was taken by Michael Cairns & is one of my favorites. It was the last number of the showcase. Each year we always ask one of the top-notch entertainers to close out the 2-day showcase with a big finale number. Then we have the entire cast of the convention to come out on stage and join them. This particular year I asked Peter Alden to close the show as Elvis. He did a fantastic job but I had no doubt. That's why I asked him. I had known Pete since 1993. He credited me with getting him his first professional Elvis gig. And he was the first celebrity impersonator I ever booked. We've been friends ever since. Our deepest sympathies go out to Krista, his son and the rest of his family. Fly high Pete.

—Greg M. Thompson, Producer of the Sunburst Convention for Celebrity Impersonators

SERGIO CASASANTA (January 25, 1958 – November 2, 2020)

Sergio Casasanta was totally dedicated to all things Ozzy Osbourne! He joined a lookalike agency in 2018 as an Ozzy tribute artist, having always been told that he looked just like the rock star. He was honored to be part of the UK lookalike industry and was very popular among other artists. He was particularly thrilled to attend conventions in the United States, where he met his American tribute 'family' and remained friends with many of them upon his return to the UK. I felt blessed to have teamed up with Sergio to perform as the husband/wife team of Sharon and Ozzy. I really miss our weekly phone chats and hearing his laughter. Sergio was a dedicated family man and brought happiness to so many people with his generosity of spirit and a huge smile. Our deepest sympathy is extended to Julie, his partner of 21 years, his 90-year old Mum Lina and his sisters.

—Caroline Bernstein, professional actor, comedian
and Sharon Osbourne Lookalike.

PAUL WILLIAM BROWN (October 14, 1954 – October 14, 2021)

For me, it's unthinkable to speak of Paul Brown in the past tense. I can't wrap my head around that. He was so full of life, funny, kind, athletic, optimistic and excited to try anything. He found opportunity in everything. He was a proud father and newly proud grandfather. Paul was an avid tennis player and the consummate salesman. Through encouraging the love of his life, his wife, Carla, in her journey as a Barbra Streisand impersonator, he discovered a passion for managing and booking talent. Paul was always full of great ideas to enhance a show, pushing it just a bit above the others, like hiring a Robert Redford impersonator to join Carla on stage for *The Way We Were*. He and Carla were a beautiful and beloved couple in the impersonator community and his absence will be acutely felt. Rest, Paul. We love you.

—Jackie Thompson, Co-Producer, Sunburst Convention for
Celebrity Impersonators

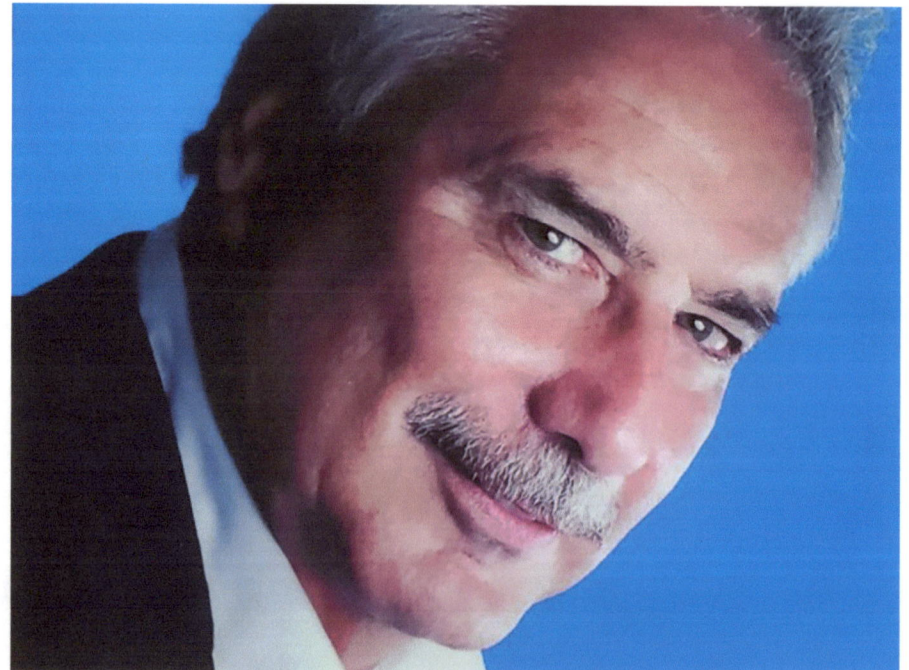

Celebrity Contact Information

Al Smith Jr. as Tiger Woods
'Tiger Woo'
Ph. (321) 231-9167 (cell)

Ashley Pitzer as Britney Spears
Email: britneytributeartist@gmail.com

Web: www.britneyonemoretime.com

- https://instagram.com/ashleypitzer_

Bettina Williams as Whoopi Goldberg
Web: www.akawhoopi.com

Betty Atchison as Cher and Lady Gaga
Ph. (407) 342-1155

Email: cheriffic@aol.com

Web: www.cheriffic.com • www.lady-gaga-impersonator.com

Bill Pantazis as George Michael
Web: www.gottabgeorgemichael.com

- www.linkedin.com/in/bill-pantazis-1152a697
- Instagram: Gotta _B_George_Michael
- Facebook: Gotta B George Michael

Billy Buchanan as Chuck Berry, Sam Cooke, Ray Charles, and Little Richard
Sharon Borneman • HYPE PR

Ph. (352) 219-1118 • email: booking@billybuchanan.org

Web: www.billybuchanan.org

Camille Terry as Marilyn Monroe
Camille Terry • Camilleon Impersonators, LLC.

Ph. *Florida*: (561) 602-0655 • *New York*: (212) 613-3136

Web: www.camilleasmarilyn.com • www.comiccamilleon.com

- www.camilleonimpersonators.com

Carla Del Villaggio as Barbra Streisand
Email: simplystreisand2@gmail.com • maineventagency@aol.com

Caroline Bernstein as Sharon Osbourne – and others
Web: www.sharonosbournelookalike.com

- Facebook: Caroline Bernstein
- Instagram: thecarolinebernstein

Chris America as Madonna
Ph. (703) 585-6072 • web: www.chrisamerica.com

C.J. Morgan as Dolly Parton

Ph. (615) 289-4815 • email: roselady5463501@aol.com

Web: www.almostdolly.com

- https://www.facebook.com/DollyPartonLookalike

Dan Schneid as Dr. Phil

Ph. (714) 812-0497 • email: drphil927@aol.com

David Babcock as Will Ferrell

Web: www.ronburgundyimpersonator.com

- www.rickybobbyimpersonator.com
- www.buddytheelfimpersonator.com

David Born as Robin Williams

Email: RobinDouble@aol.com

Web: www.RobinWilliamsImpersonator.com

- www.imdb.com/name/nm0097022/

Deborah Smith Ford as Trinity from *The Matrix*

Web: AlliesAdventures.com

- Deborah Smith Ford at: IMDb.com and YouTube.com

Eric Finch as Snoop Dogg

Ph. (562) 550-8700 • email: contact@ericfinchentertainment.com

Web: ericfinchentertainment.com

George Kane as Hugh Hefner

Ph. (239) 994-8989 • email: gemo2@aol.com

Web: www.hughhefnerlookalike.com

Greg Thompson as Andy Warhol, Austin Powers, Jack Sparrow, and Santa

Ph. (407) 226-9088 • email: greg@vagabondtroupe.com

Web: www.vagabondtroupe.com

Gregg Williams as Clint Eastwood

Ph. (408) 439-1980 • web: www.facebook.com/gregg.williams.3194

Jack Bullard as Jack Nicholson

Ph. (719) 216-5220

Email: jacknicholsonimpersonator@yahoo.com

Web: www.jacknicholsonimpersonator.com

Jamie Pagett as Walter White

Tel: 01889 502508 • Mobile: 07966 264725

Email: jamie@ashcroftpark.co.uk

Web: www.walterwhitelookalike.com • www.ashcroftpark.co.uk

Address: Falcon Ridge, Bramshall, Uttoxeter, ST14 8SQ

Jed Duvall as Paul McCartney

Web: www.jedduvall.com

Jeff Richards as Tim McGraw

Email: jeff@twinmcgraw.com • web: www.twinmcgraw.com

Jennifer Ramsey as Lucy, Liza, Judge Judy, and Bette Davis

Ph. (239) 514-4055 • web: www.RamseysReplicas.com

- www.JenniferRamsey.com

Joe Passion as Jerry Lee Lewis

Web: www.joepassion.com

John Di Domenico as President Donald Trump

Ph. (702) 932-8675 • email: john@johnnyd.net

Web: www.johnnyd.net

John Morgan as President George W. Bush

Ph. (407) 376-9974 • email: John@JohnCMorgan.com

Web: www.johncmorgan.com

Johnny D. Miller as The Colonel

Web: www.besserentertainment.com

- www.colsandersimpersonator.com

Johnny Moroko as Mick Jagger

Ph. (209) 614-4855 • email: johnnymoroko@yahoo.com

Julie Myers as Stevie Nicks

Email: julie@nearlynicks.com • web: www.nearlynicks.com

Keith George as Boy George

Ph. +447962365846 • email: keith@boygeorgeexperience.com

Web: Instagram BoyGeorgeExperience

- FaceBook Keith George - The Boy George Experience

Lawrence Calvin as Steve Harvey

Email: afann4life@yahoo.com • web: tributetolegends.net

Mark Staggs as Festus from the Television Series Gunsmoke

Email: smstaggs1@gmail.com • web: Facebook; Mark Staggs Comedy

Matt Cordell as Jason Aldean

Ph. (865) 591-6138 • email: mattcordell21@yahoo.com

Address: P.O. Box 6324, Sevierville, TN 37864

Michael "Wally" Walter as Don Rickles

Ph. (360) 584-8885 • email: mikewallywalter@hotmail.com

Web: www.donricklesimpersonator.com • www.mikewallywalter.net

Mira Tzur as Melania Trump

Web: www.miratzur.com • www.melaniaanddonaldtrumpdoubles.com

Monica Leamy as Gwen Stefani

Email: subliminaldoubt@gmail.com

Web: SubliminalDoubt on Facebook and Instagram

Natalie Black as Adele

Email: Adeletributeact@gmail.com • web: www.adele-tribute.net

Rhys Whittock as Prince Harry

Ph. +44 79 808 188 76 • email: theprinceharrylookalike@gmail.com

Web: www.princeharrylookalike.com

- Facebook: The Prince Harry Lookalike

- Instagram: @theprinceharrylookalike

Ronnie Rodriguez as Johnny Depp

Web: www.ronnierodriguez.com

Samira as Tina Turner

Ph. (800) 958-3963 • web: www.trulytina.com

Sarah Mhlanga as Meghan Markle

Email: Agent jabzz@raiefilms.com

Web: www.sarahmhlanga.com

- Instagram www.instagram.com/sarahmhlangaofficial/

Scott Jordan as Justin Timberlake, Ricky Nelson, and Luke Bryan

Ph. (407) 432-9020 • email: tributetrilogyshow@yahoo.com

Web: www.tributetrilogyshow.com

Scott Mason as Dame Edna

Ph. (302) 456-0311 • email: hirethedame@yahoo.com

Web: www.hirethedame.com

Sean Banks as Obama

Email: sean_is_barack@yahoo.com

Web: www.sean@presidentobamaimpersonator.com

Shannon Michaels as Bret Michaels

Ph. (608) 728-4489 • email: shannonmichaels1@yahoo.com

Web: www.shannonmichaels.net

Sharon Holmes as Martha Stewart

Ph. (714) 348-8977 • email: sharon@sharonasmartha.com

Web: www.sharonasmartha.com

Steve Edenbo as Thomas Jefferson

Ph. +1 (323) 850-0825 • email: contact@mirrorimages.co

Web: www.mirrorimages.co

Steve Weber as Forrest Gump

Steve Weber • 610 N First St, #5-305, Hamilton, MT 59840

Ph. (406) 396-4611 • email: Steve@speakinggump.com

Web: www.speakinggump.com

Taylor Copenhaver as Eminem

Web: www.twitter.com/ActorDude07

- www.taylormathers.tumblr.com

Ted Torres Martin as Elvis Presley

Email: elvis32837@yahoo.com • web: www.revisitedelvis.com

Terry Lee Goffee as Johnny Cash

Tony Cee Associates • Ph. (315) 735-9959

Web: www.terryleegoffee.com

Vic Vaga as Rod Stewart

Email: vicvaga@rocketmail.com • web: www.vegasrod.com

Wally Sheppard as Kris Kristofferson

Email: kristoffersonequipped@gmail.com

About the Authors

C.J. MORGAN AND JACK BULLARD have more in common than being married to each other; the husband-wife team both work as celebrity impersonators; Jack is a dead-ringer for film icon Jack Nicholson while C.J. is an award-winning Dolly Parton Tribute Artist. They met at the Sunburst Conference for Professional Celebrity Impersonators, held yearly in Orlando, Florida and have now branched out into motivational speaking. Their keynote address is part entertainment, part information and lots of stories about what it is really like to be in this fascinating business. They answer some of the curious, often funny, often personal questions people ask regarding their unusual occupation. Now they have published a book that includes many of their friends in the business. *Daily Doubles: Celebrity Impersonators* offers a brief glimpse into the lives of the entertainers who are the "next best thing" to the real deal.

The writing of this book was no easy task. C.J. says, "We have many friends in the industry and knew it would be difficult to pick and choose whose stories to put forth. So, we developed an informal editorial board consisting of agents, producers, theater owners and some of the top-tier, award-winning artists who have already achieved excellence in their field; entertainers we already knew would be included. Their suggestions went far beyond those covered within these pages so this is by no means a comprehensive collection, but it is a taste of the cream of the crop. Some of the artists here are relatively new to the scene; others have had years of experience. Some are lookalikes only, others offer full tribute shows. Despite the competitiveness and egocentricity that is at times present in show business, all represented here offer talent, experience, professionalism, hard work and a positive attitude. There will be more entertainers featured in our next book. In the meantime, we hope you enjoy meeting our friends and hearing their stories."

www.ingramcontent.com/pod-product-compliance
Lightning Source LLC
Chambersburg PA
CBHW041421160426

42812CB00091B/2663